GOD'S CURRENCY

by Neil Kennedy

Neil Kennedy Ministries Group
82 Plantation Pointe
Fairhope, AL 36532
www.NeilKennedyMinistries.com

God's Currency

Neil Kennedy Ministries Group
82 Plantation Pointe, Fairhope, AL 36532,
www.NeilKennedyMinistries.com

DEDICATION

This book is dedicated to my wife, Kay,
who never wavers in the face of challenge,
whose kindness is like the kiss of beauty itself,
whose faith inspires me to know Christ more,
and to my three amazing children,
Alexandra, Chase, and Courtney.
I love you.

TABLE OF CONTENTS

INTRODUCTION:
THE BLESSING

⌇

LIVING UNDER GOD'S
OPEN HEAVEN

1 INTRODUCTION
GOD'S PROMISE OF AN OPEN HEAVEN

*The Lord will open the heavens, the storehouse of
his bounty, to send rain on your land in season
and to bless all the work of your hands. You will
lend to many nations but will borrow from none.*
Deuteronomy 28:12 NIV

Close your eyes and just imagine standing under a starry
sky, lifting your hands toward Heaven in worship, and then
hearing the unmistakable voice of God saying, *"I will open
up my storehouse of bounty. My wealth is yours for the
asking. What do you want from me?"*

As a young boy growing up in Oklahoma, I loved to go out
into the open pastures at night, find a comfortable place to
lie down, and pretend to visit each star that my eyes would
fixate upon. I would focus on one star after another, each
one seemingly deeper out in space. It was during those
isolated times that God first began to instruct me. That is
when I first understood the vastness of God's strength and
ability. The Creator of the Universe commissioned those
stars. His power and wealth are immeasurable.

*When I consider your heavens, the work of your
fingers, the moon and the stars, which you have
set in place, what is man that you are mindful of*

him, the son of man that you care for him?
                              Psalm 8:3-4 NIV

When God said, *"Let there be Light,"* light began. To this
day, light continues to expand at its own speed, never to
stop or slow its pace. God is a God of continual increase
and expansion.

That's the image I have in my mind when I read the
blessing promised in Deuteronomy 28:12. I see the
vastness of God's creation opened up for mankind.

**The Lord will open the heavens...to send rain on
your land in season....**
                              Deuteronomy 28:12a NIV

This blessing from God promises abundance and due timing
of rain. The promise of rain is a promise of prosperity. A
lack of rain brings famine, starvation and death. Famine is
the epitome of poverty. I have tasted the sting of poverty in
my life. It once oppressed me. I don't like the bitter pill of
lack. When I visit countries burdened with poverty, I weep
at the misery it causes. I am repulsed by the stench of
insufficiency.

If you have ever seen the effects of true poverty, you know
that **it can't be the desire of God for mankind.** Man was
made in the image of God. Man has too much dignity
encoded in his DNA to live in destitution.

God's promise of an abundance of rain is a promise of
prosperity. When you know how to harness the power of
rain, you can enjoy tremendous rewards. God's resources,
when properly managed, bring wealth and reserves.

On the other hand, even a natural resource, such as rain, can
be destructive if it is not controlled or channeled. One of
the simple differences between developed countries and
what we know as "Third World" countries is the
infrastructure created within them to harness the power of

rain. If you don't know how to manage the earth's resources, you will live in poverty.

Likewise, when you know how to harness the power of God's resources—His currency—you will enjoy its rewards. But left uncontrolled, over-abundance will become a destructive force in your life.

Many examples of destruction resulting from over abundance are found in the myriad of stories involving what I call "Sudden Wealth Syndrome," or "SWS." Sudden Wealth Syndrome happens when someone wins the lottery or finds overnight stardom.

_____  _____

Godly prosperity is not the accumulation of money.

_____  _____

The vast majority of professional athletes, television and movie stars, and lottery winners have uncontrolled wealth. They are flooded with more money than they have the wisdom to manage. Over the course of time, their lack of wisdom eventually costs them all that they have. It's a fact that the average lottery winner is bankrupt within 48 months of their windfall.

> *The blessing of the LORD, it maketh rich, and he addeth no sorrow with it.*
>   *Proverbs 10:22*

Godly prosperity is not the accumulation of money.

Listen to me carefully, money is a *fruit* of the prosperous person—it is not his *root.* When I think of prosperity, I think in terms of *purpose*—not money. In other words, a prosperous man is a man who has what he needs to accomplish the assignment of his purpose on this earth.

I must admit I have always been attracted to the prosperity message. I've read hundreds of books concerning wealth building. Many were good. Some were foolish. However, I have never heard what I am about to share with you in the following chapters. If you read this book you will discover this one central truth: **God does *not* deal with you in money.**

Cold, hard, cash is not the commodity that God uses to provide for His children. He does deal with us in things that *lead to wealth.* But He doesn't rain down pennies—or dollars—from Heaven.

The enemy has been able to rob godly people of the real truth of prosperity. The majority of the Body of Christ recoils at the sound of the word "prosperity" because their mind is conditioned to equate money with prosperity. The error is in the emphasis.

For every mile of road there are two miles of ditch. You can be in the ditch with a poverty mentality, or you can be in the ditch of erroneous prosperity teaching. Either way you are still in the ditch and not on the true path of God's Word.

I stated in my book, *Grace to Grow—The Seven Laws Which Govern Divine Increase And Order,* that "there are those who have meaning without means and there are those who have means without meaning." Neither condition is God's plan.

Webster's Dictionary defines the word *currency* as *"something in circulation as a medium of exchange."* **God's currency brings His children the blessings of prosperity through many different channels of exchange.** Banknotes are not the legal tender of Heaven.

> *But remember the LORD your God, for it is he who gives you the ability to produce wealth, and so confirms his covenant, which he swore to your*

forefathers, as it is today.
                                              Deuteronomy 8:18 NIV

My prayer is that by the end of this book you will know how to deal in the currency of God. You will flow freely in the different modes of exchange in His kingdom. I pray that you will gain a position of dominance over money. Money—or the lack thereof—will not control you, but you will learn to master it.

This book is written not only to *inspire* you to believe that God desires for you to prosper but also to *empower* you with an understanding of His system of prosperity.

...You will lend to many nations but will borrow from none.
                                              Deuteronomy 28:12b NIV

The end result of an open Heaven is that you will be a lender and will have no need to borrow. Borrowing money is not forbidden in scripture, but we are warned against it. Living in debt is not God's highest and best for you. Don't settle into the trap that you can't enjoy the life you want without credit to pay for it. The Bible says the borrower is a slave to the lender. Which one do you prefer to be? I have determined that my family will owe no one anything but the continued debt of love.

The following chapters of this book will open up your understanding to help you take your place under an open Heaven with your hands raised high in the air, your feet spread apart and your head lifted in a position of receiving. Read this book with a new sense of destiny and an anticipation that finally, you will be empowered to prosper in a godly fashion through God's currency—not coveting or being filled with greed—but truly prospering as God intended.

1 GOD-GIVEN TALENT

> *So God created man in his own image, in the*
> *image of God he created him; male and female he*
> *created them.*
>
> *Genesis 1:27*

God is a creative god.

You are created in His image. The word *image* means
"shadowed likeness." Within you is a shadowed likeness
of the Creator. Within you is the ability to be creative.
Your creativity is a shadow of the creative power of God.

> *The LORD God formed the man from the dust of*
> *the ground and breathed into his nostrils the*
> *breath of life, and the man became a living being.*
>
> *Genesis 2:7*

God's breath—His Spirit—resides within you.

In other words, your existence is not an evolutionary step of
accidents, nor is it a random occurrence of chance. You
were designed in the image of your Creator.

> *Before I formed you in the womb I knew you,*
> *before you were born I set you apart....*
>
> *Jeremiah 1:5*

You were birthed with expectation and excitement. You are set apart for God's purpose. Your destiny awaits your discovery.

Within you is ability, talent, skill, knowledge, craft and wisdom—the gifts—or the "currency" of God. When you discover them, train them, enlarge your use of them and master them, man will exchange his currency (dollars) for your gifts.

The inheritance of God is within your spirit.

You must understand that **your provision in life does not come from chasing after money but in fulfilling your God-given purpose.** When you go about the business of completing God's assignments for your life, money will simply come to you as a by-product. Man will pour into your lap the necessary means to fulfill God's plans for you.

Have you ever dreamed of what you would do with enormous amounts of money?

Be honest. We all have. The conclusion of my fantasy is always that I would have all of my base needs supplied so that I could be completely free to fulfill my purpose. That is God's plan for all of His children.

Where most people miss it is that they spend their lives chasing after sufficiency. Each week they go to work, spending hours pursuing the interests of others so that on the weekend they can have a day or two to pursue their own personal interests. Each week ends the same way. They deposit their paychecks, and then spend hours writing out checks of their own to cover their living expenses for that week. Ninety-eight percent of people never change their routine. Their theme song is *"I owe, I owe, so off to work I go!"*

Solomon summed it up like this: *"What an evil under the sun! What does a man gain from his constant toil and work*

only to hand it to someone who didn't work for it?"
(Ecclesiastes 6:1-2 author's paraphrase)

Most people live their entire lives barely making a living rather than fulfilling their God-given assignments on earth.

That is not God's plan.

Satan has somehow bound us to a rat race of mere existence. We work, eat and sleep only to become workaholics, gluttons and over-consumers.

But deep within us is something extremely more valuable than the ability to just get by. Yet, it requires a fundamental paradigm shift in our thinking to break out of that mode of living.

_____ ⚭ _____

Provision doesn't come from chasing after money.

_____ ⚭ _____

You must understand what your purpose is and what is on deposit within you in order to finance it. You must truly believe that it is God's desire to prosper you. He delights in prospering the person who is faithful to His purpose.

Jesus teaches the Parable of the Talents to explain God's way of thinking.

> *For the kingdom of heaven is as a man travelling into a far country, who called his own servants, and delivered unto them his goods. And unto one he gave five talents, to another two, and to another one; to every man according to his several ability; and straightway took his journey. Then he that had received the five talents went and traded with the same, and made them other five talents. And likewise he that had received two, he also gained other two. But he that had received one went and*

*digged in the earth, and hid his lord's money.
After a long time the lord of those servants
cometh, and reckoneth with them. And so he that
had received five talents came and brought other
five talents, saying, Lord, thou deliveredst unto me
five talents: behold, I have gained beside them
five talents more. His lord said unto him, Well
done, thou good and faithful servant: thou hast
been faithful over a few things, I will make thee
ruler over many things: enter thou into the joy of
thy lord. He also that had received two talents
came and said, Lord, thou deliveredst unto me two
talents: behold, I have gained two other talents
beside them. His lord said unto him, Well done,
good and faithful servant; thou hast been faithful
over a few things, I will make thee ruler over
many things: enter thou into the joy of thy lord.
Then he which had received the one talent came
and said, Lord, I knew thee that thou art an hard
man, reaping where thou hast not sown, and
gathering where thou hast not strawed: And I was
afraid, and went and hid thy talent in the earth:
lo, there thou hast that is thine. His lord
answered and said unto him, Thou wicked and
slothful servant, thou knewest that I reap where I
sowed not, and gather where I have not strawed:
Thou oughtest therefore to have put my money to
the exchangers, and then at my coming I should
have received mine own with usury. Take
therefore the talent from him, and give it unto him
which hath ten talents. For unto every one that
hath shall be given, and he shall have abundance:
but from him that hath not shall be taken away
even that which he hath. And cast ye the
unprofitable servant into outer darkness: there*

shall be weeping and gnashing of teeth.
                        Matthew 25:14-30

Each man was entrusted with the master's talents according to his proven skill. The master invested in each man's ability. The servants weren't given any more or less than they had proved themselves able to handle. And when the master returned from his journey, he asked for an accounting, or an audit of the books. Each man had to justify and give an account for the investments that he had made.

The servant who received five talents gained five more. The servant who received two talents gained two more.

This is an important point: By showing themselves faithful in their current abilities, they doubled those abilities. The five-talent servant was measured from that point on as a ten-talent servant. The two-talent servant was then measured as a four-talent servant.

The master was ecstatic with his praise for the two faithful servants. He gave them both promotions and invited them to share in his joy. You can imagine the celebration. This was a company party where the employees were celebrating a great period of profits.

Obviously, the tone of the story changes dramatically when the unfaithful servant who merely maintained what the master gave him came on the scene.

Notice the obnoxious attitude of the servant from the outset. He actually blamed the master for his poor performance. Fear paralyzed the servant from taking action and he unjustly judged the motivation of the master when he said, *"I knew thee that thou art an hard man, reaping where thou hast not sown, and gathering where thou hast not strawed: And I was afraid...."*

Pay attention to this principle: **You will never excel if your motivation is fear.**

Most people do not realize how closely their thinking every day resembles this servant's attitude. His focus was on maintenance, not performance. He was unfaithful because he was controlled by fear. This servant was unfruitful because he misjudged his master's desire for increase.

The master replied that at the very minimum, the servant should have drawn interest from his investment.

The very least that God expects is what the world is willing to pay. But God expects much more from His faithful servants.

_____  _____

You will never excel if your motivation is fear.

_____  _____

You have God-given talents on loan from Heaven. If you are faithful to the talents and giftings He has given you, you will multiply your present abilities. If you are unfaithful with the talents God has loaned to you for increase, one day you will find that you have lost the very abilities that you once possessed.

When you work to excel and increase your God-given talents, man will bring you his currency in exchange for your expertise. And as you are faithful to honor the Lord with your financial increase He will, in turn, expand your abilities and His investment in you. The process is a never-ending circle of blessing for the faithful and obedient servants of God.

2 GOD IS NOT A COUNTERFEITER

God will not counterfeit man's currency to answer your prayers. He doesn't have a printing press rolling out "dead Presidents" on pieces of paper! When you pray for provision, God is not going to rain money into your lap or shower gold down onto your head.

Years ago, at my first church, a visitor who attended approach me following a service. He said, "Pastor, I received a letter from a sweepstakes with my name listed as one of only five people who could win one million dollars. Would you agree with me that I will win this prize? I promise that I will give 10% of it to your church."

I turned him down.

I knew that the sweepstakes company had deceived him by printing his name on a paper saying that he was one of only a few people in the running to win this contest. This man was deceived to think that God would manipulate man's gimmickry to bless him. On top of that, I'd never seen this man before. It was obvious that he wasn't a practicing believer. Him giving a tenth of his income to the church would have never happened. (If you're not faithful in little, you won't be faithful in plenty.)

God will not bless you with riches by rigging a lottery or a sweepstakes! If you do win some sort of contest, you can be sure it was a random occurrence and not the manipulation of God.

God will not enrich His children by fraud.

Occasionally, schools will send out their students to raise money for various projects. My own children know that I will not buy raffle tickets to win something. I will make a donation to a school, but I won't purchase "chances" to win an item. I believe that's no different than a lottery—it's all gambling.

Friend, it's evil what many states have done to establish government-sponsored lotteries in America. The truth is that a lottery is nothing but a deceptive "tax" on the poor. It's wrong, unethical and criminal. Yet people who can't afford to throw away their money do it every day in the hopes that they'll strike it rich.

> *The Lord will open the heavens, the storehouse of his bounty...to bless all the work of your hands.*
> *Deuteronomy 28:12b NIV*

God isn't working some spooky magic on your "lucky" number or on some horse in a race.

No. The Bible is clear. It says that He will bless *the work of your hands*.

While I attended Bible College, I worked as a salesman at a car wash. The company wanted to motivate the salesmen by offering a trip to Las Vegas as a prize. Included in the trip were two airline tickets, hotel accommodations and several hundred dollars in cash to use to gamble in the casinos there.

After a few weeks into the contest my sales were so far ahead of all the other salesmen that no one could catch me. I won the contest, and I promptly rejected the prize of the trip. I simply asked for the money. I didn't want the appearance of me going to Las Vegas to gamble to hinder my testimony among my co-workers. My decision seemed so outrageous to my coworkers that many of them began to question me about my motivations in life. Because of my bold stand and testimony, I won the respect of my peers and led several of them to the Lord during the time that I worked there. *(I'll tell you more of what I learned at the car wash in a later chapter.)*

I was enriched by the work of my hands.

God isn't working some spooky magic on a horse in a race.

If God is going to bless you it will not be by manipulating man's silly little games. It will be through *His system* of prosperity. Don't be distracted by the schemes of satan.

> *He that tilleth his land shall be satisfied with bread: but he that followeth vain persons is void of understanding.*
> *Proverbs 12:11*

God will bless the work of your hands!

> *Give, and it shall be given unto you; good measure, pressed down, and shaken together, and running over, shall men give into your bosom.*
> *Luke 6:38*

Who will give into your bosom?

Men will.

Why will men give to you?

Men give what they have in their hands for one reason—to make an exchange. *(I'll explain later how the Law of Exchange works.)*

Don't attempt to bring God down to man's level by asking Him to deal with you in earthly currency. That's ridiculous.

Let me illustrate this principle further.

My wife's great-grandfather, Mr. Everett, was a very wealthy man. He had thousands of acres and he employed hundreds of men to work his land, timber and turpentine stills. For convenience, he opened regional stores where his employees could purchase items. For the payroll, Mr. Everett issued private currency—wooden coins printed with his name on them. Employees were free to use them in his stores.

Although the wooden coins were valuable in his small circle, they were not valuable to the United States Government. The government would not deal with Mr. Everett or his employees in "Everett currency." It was inferior to their real currency.

The same is true for us. God is not going to deal with us in the limited currency of men.

If you've asked God for money, you've asked Him for an inferior medium of exchange. Instead, you need to ask Him to deal with you in His currency—not the currency of men.

Think about how silly it is to chase after money. People who covet riches are so deceived. Many men run after what they believe to be the ultimate manifestation of wealth—gold. But think about it. Gold is the *asphalt* of Heaven! (Revelation 21:21)

> *Wilt thou set thine eyes upon that which is not?*
> *For riches certainly make themselves wings; they*

fly away as an eagle toward heaven.
                              Proverbs 23:5

If you glance at riches they fly away. *(Maybe that's why our dollars and coins are marked with an eagle.)* Today the U.S. Dollar is no longer valued by the standard of gold and silver.

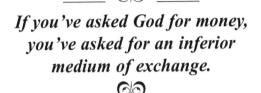

If you've asked God for money, you've asked for an inferior medium of exchange.

Our dollar floats on a value placed upon it by the confidence of men. If people feel depressed about the economy, the value of our money goes down. If people feel optimistic about the economy, the value goes up. That's why the entire world pauses while the Federal Reserve decides what the value of a dollar is every three months. In one fleeting moment economists manipulate what our currency is worth based on people's feelings!

> *They shall cast their silver in the streets, and their gold shall be removed: their silver and their gold shall not be able to deliver them in the day of the wrath of the LORD: they shall not satisfy their souls, neither fill their bowels: because it is the stumblingblock of their iniquity.*
>   ***Ezekiel 7:19***

Do you realize how unstable money really is?

Since I was graduated from high school in 1980, one dollar is now worth the equivalent of only forty cents.

Get this idea out of your head! The accumulation of money is not the primary goal of your life!

The only reason you need money is to successfully make an exchange. The goal of life is to fulfill your assignment of purpose. Prosperity means that your journey toward your destiny will go well with you. More than likely you will need some form of support. But money is not the ultimate goal! It's simply a means of exchange to achieve the God-given design for your life.

Money in and of itself is limited, insecure and fleeting. It makes a terrible master, as we will discover in the next chapter.

3 DUPLICITY: YOU CAN'T SERVE TWO MASTERS

Ye cannot serve God and mammon.
Matthew 6:24

A double minded man is unstable in all his ways.
James 1:8

Pause for a moment to put this in perspective: Money is a horrible master but an excellent servant. When you place an emotive property on money, it takes on a spirit—a demonic spirit.

For the love of money is the root of all evil: which while some coveted after, they have erred from the faith, and pierced themselves through with many sorrows.

I Timothy 6:10

Paul did not teach what some have erroneously said, that "money is the root of all evil." He taught that *"the love of money is the root of all evil."* (The American Standard Version says, *"the love of money is a root of all kinds of evil."*) When you attach love—the thing that belongs to God alone, according to Deuteronomy 6:5—to money you have personified it to become "Mammon." You've made a god out of it.

If you love money, you are deceived. If you think that money is a good god, you are mistaken. History has plenty of examples of people who had lots of money without any peace.

When compared to the dignity of your high calling, seeking money is degrading. Setting your heart on obtaining wealth is beneath the purpose God has for you.

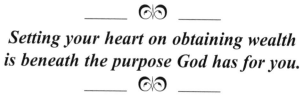

Setting your heart on obtaining wealth is beneath the purpose God has for you.

Therefore take no thought, saying, What shall we eat? or, What shall we drink? or, Wherewithal shall we be clothed? (For after all these things do the Gentiles seek:) for your heavenly Father knoweth that ye have need of all these things.
Matthew 6:31-32

It is humiliating for man to spend his days chasing after the things of this earth. It's insane to be possessed by the drive to accumulate things just for the sake of accumulation.

Naked I came from my mother's womb, and naked I will depart.

Job 1:21

You can't take anything that you gathered on this earth with you when you die—that is, unless you make an exchange of currency—unless you exchange your earthly, temporal currency for the Heavenly, eternal currency of God.

Store up for yourselves treasures in heaven, where moth and rust do not destroy, and where thieves do not break in and steal.

Matthew 6:20

You must become single-minded when it comes to the pursuit of your life. If you focus on money, your pursuit will cause you to chase after the wind. You may gather it up and even harness it for a while, but sooner or later, it will leave your grasp.

However, if you pursue the kingdom of God, you'll discover that your storehouse is full and secure, and your treasures are everlasting.

In his book, *More Than A Hobby,* (Nashville, TN: Nelson Business, 2005), author David Green explains how he became one of the wealthiest men in America, ranking as number 133 on Forbes' list of billionaires.

This self-made merchant began selling picture frames with an initial investment of only $600. As a minister's son, David grew up recognizing the hand of God upon his life. He explains that it is not *how much* he can increase, but *why* he should increase that determines a man's level of prosperity.

David Green's pursuit is not money. His focus is to honor God in every area of his business. Money is simply a medium he uses in exchange for God's currency. In 2005, he purchased more than fifty million dollars worth of real estate so that churches could expand their ministries.

A few years ago, his representatives called me while I was planting a second church in Orlando, Florida. I had been praying about purchasing a facility that had formerly housed the television program *American Gladiators.* Mr. Green made a generous offer to purchase the building on my behalf, and although the offer was not accepted, I learned to appreciate this faithful man of God and his wisdom concerning money.

Being focused is vital when it comes to handling your finances. **If you cannot focus on anything but the "how much" of your money, you will become its servant.**

> *Ye ask, and receive not, because ye ask amiss, that ye may consume it upon your lusts.*
>
> *James 4:3*

When you ask for money you're asking amiss, meaning that you ask *in a wrong manner.* The word *amiss* in the Greek language is the same word used for *"sick," "ill,"* or *"miserable."* Asking God for something in a wrong manner is compared to when your body is not functioning properly, like having a sick feeling or an upset stomach.

_____ ☉☉ _____

If you focus on money, your pursuit will cause you to chase after the wind.
_____ ☉☉ _____

When you pray for the consumption of your fleshly desires, your prayer is unhealthy, ill, and nauseating. God will not give money to you to satisfy your lusts. But when you pray to receive God's currency, you receive a *way to obtain* or *a system to provide* true wealth.

> *And the cares of this world, and the deceitfulness of riches, and the lusts of other things entering in, choke the word, and it becometh unfruitful.*
>
> *Mark 4:19*

Jesus teaches that three things suffocate the Word:

1. The cares of this world—The word *care* literally means *"anxiety,"* or "*to be drawn in another direction."* It is a direction completely opposed to the Word of God.

2. The deceitfulness of riches—*Deceitfulness* means *"to be led astray, to wander, to stagger,"* or *"to be led off course."*

3. The lusts of other things—This means that you develop an obsession for things, a very strong

desire, or even become a *"maniac"* (without reason) for things.

God is not interested in satisfying your lust for pleasure, but He is concerned about the fulfillment of your purpose.

The world's idea that pleasure and happiness are the chief aims in life is *hedonism.* God will have nothing to do with it. The spirit behind this kind of pursuit is the same spirit that is behind sexual sin and adultery. In fact, James goes on to describe it this way.

> *Ye adulterers and adulteresses, know ye not that the friendship of the world is enmity with God? Whosoever therefore will be a friend of the world is the enemy of God.*
>
> *James 4:4*

If your pursuit is communion (friendship) with this world's system, your pursuit is in direct opposition to God. It is the same spirit behind adultery. It is unfaithfulness and the breaking of your covenant with the Lord.

> *But seek ye first the kingdom of God, and his righteousness; and all these things shall be added unto you.*
>
> *Matthew 6:33*

Don't waste your time and efforts praying for or pursuing after money. God has a better way and a better system of provision in store for you. Prosperity will be a by-product of your pursuit of the kingdom of God.

4 ERROR THROUGH EMPHASIS

The man who fears God will avoid all extremes.
Ecclesiastes 7:18 NIV

I said before that many people are hostile toward the teaching of prosperity because of error through emphasis.

Ministers oftentimes teach and illustrate from their unique perspectives. Unknowingly, when a minister uses the way that he receives money to describe God's system of prosperity, it's not usually applicable to the common man.

Anyone who receives instruction in the word must share all good things with his instructor.
Galatians 6:6 NIV

A minister receives money because he teaches the Word. **The Word is a currency of God.**

If a minister shares an example of someone he didn't know coming up and giving him money, or of purchasing a car for him, or a watch, or whatever, the minister may not have known the giver, but the giver knew him. More than likely the person received teaching from that minister. In some way that person knew and felt led to give to that man of God.

This has happened often in my ministry. One day I was mowing my lawn when a car pulled up to the curb. A young couple that had just begun to attend my church approached me and handed me a check for $1,200. I hardly knew them.

More than likely, you don't have people handing you checks for $1,200 while you're mowing your lawn. This couple said that they were praying about a need in their own lives and felt prompted to give when they thought of my work as a pastor.

Down through the years, I have received seven different cars from people for my ministry. Each time I received a car, it was a result of someone knowing me or receiving the Word from my ministry. The minister receives things this way because this is one system of God's currency.

But a plumber doesn't receive money that way. When a plumber asks God for provision, God favors him in his work to receive more plumbing jobs. **Work is a currency of God.** Or he may receive an idea of how to do his job better or more efficiently. Then he can teach this idea to others who might pay him for the instruction. **An idea is a currency of God.**

Unfortunately, some laypeople have heard ministers teach on prosperity and have quit their jobs saying, "God will supply all my needs." They end up shipwrecked in the faith because they presumed a position for which they were not qualified.

The error comes from the focus of ministerial perspective. A minister serves in the system of God through the Levitical principle. The Levites were set apart from their brothers to be ministers of the Lord. The currency of man came to them solely based upon the faithfulness of others to bring it to them.

Men give to me because they have a relationship with my ministry. Early on, only family members and a few close friends knew me and trusted the call of God upon my life. Now thousands of people have received from my teaching, therefore, thousands have a relationship with me through my ministry.

Unfortunately, some laypeople have heard ministers teach on prosperity and have quit their jobs.

When I planted my second church, I had a team of young ministers who joined me in the work. *(Planting a church is difficult work. It requires tremendous sacrifice and faith.)* I put myself in agreement with my team members that their needs would be met by their own faith, not by mine. In other words, my team needed to develop their own faith and their own networks of support. As a church plant, I knew we would not have the budget to finance them. All agreed.

I encouraged them to contact their family members and friends who believed in the call of God upon their lives and who would invest in their ministries. Some did so and were able to receive a base salary out of the generosity of their friends.

My financial base was more established than my younger team members. I didn't contact my relatives or friends; I contacted those associated with my proven ministry. I began to travel and teach others and my support remained solid. I developed a seminar called *The Seven Laws Which Govern Divine Increase And Order* and began to teach it all over the nation. I would preach on Sunday mornings in my own pulpit and then leave immediately after for the airport to fly out to preach somewhere each Sunday night in another church. I held leadership training sessions on Mondays, traveled back home on Tuesdays and repeated that schedule each week.

Although I received compensation for my travel and offerings for my teaching, I poured that money into our church, covering its expenses for the first two-and-a-half years. I was generous to give to my team members when I had the funds to do so. Although I earned this money through my efforts, I prospered in order to fulfill my purpose, not to enrich myself.

One of my team members didn't have a support base of friends or family. He worked as a salesman to raise his support. It was difficult for him to understand why God would supply my needs through offerings and through my teaching while he had to work a secular job.

Yet even the Apostle Paul worked at times in secular employment to fulfill God's assignment for him.

> *And because he (Paul) was of the same craft, he abode with them, and wrought: for by their occupation they were tentmakers.*
>
> *Acts 18:3*

Ministers do a disservice to the Body of Christ by emphasizing how they receive money rather than teaching how God's currency works in the lives of average believers. Because of a lack of understanding, many of God's children get their eyes on "supernatural" provision and off of God's real plan.

When you understand God's currency, you will have a superior system of supply. You won't chase fantasies and become involved in get-rich-quick-schemes.

Years ago, a man in my church was involved in a multi-level-marketing system. He did very well. He approached me with an offer to help me financially. He wanted to put my name in his "down-line" to "bless" me. I considered it as a possible means of provision. At the time, I wasn't making much money and reasoned that this might have been a way for God to bless me. I was naive. I should have known better.

What I didn't realize was that I was transferring my influence to him by allowing my name to be used. **Influence is God's currency.**

> *A good name is more desirable than great riches;*
> *to be esteemed is better than silver or gold.*
> *Proverbs 22:1*

If I had taken the time to seek wisdom, I would have seen his true motive. If he really wanted to bless me all he had to do was pay tithes on his income. But he didn't. In fact, I later received a word from God to warn him saying, *"Remember the Lord who gives you the ability to produce wealth."* When I obeyed the Lord and spoke to him about what God had said, he didn't receive it. He didn't receive the Word of God because he felt I was in a position "beneath" him. I was in his "down-line."

I withdrew from the relationship, and later this man lost everything—his business, his family, his home, his reputation and his faith.

Many ministers and churches have forfeited their good names for schemes to produce finances.

A few years ago a phone company approached the Christian community with a marketing scheme. Their deal was that if a ministry promoted their specific phone product, that particular ministry would receive a 10% tithe (a kick-back) of the phone company's profits. But when customers had problems with this phone company and their shoddy performance, guess who they would call—the church or ministry that recruited them to sign up! The names and reputations of the ministries involved were then confused with the bad phone company.

God's system of financing His Church is established through the tithes and free-will offerings of believers. A story in the life of Abraham beautifully illustrates this principle.

Influence is God's currency.

Abraham won his nephew Lot back from captivity in battle after Lot had been kidnapped. The King of Sodom approached Abraham to reward him. Abraham's reply is interesting to read.

> *...I will not take from a thread even to a shoelatchet, and that I will not take any thing that is thine, lest thou shouldest say, I have made Abram rich.*
>
> *Genesis 14:23*

Abraham refused to receive his wealth from a homosexual king. Abraham protected his good name, valuing his influence and the reputation of God as his Provider.

The Word of the Lord came to Abraham afterward and said:

> *Fear not, Abram: I am thy shield, and thy exceeding great reward.*
>
> *Genesis 15:1*

God reassured Abraham. Abraham's confidence was in God's promise not in man's schemes.

When satan sees a man devoting himself to serve the Lord and trusting in God's currency, he often devises a scheme to obligate that man financially. When a believer begins to tithe, the devil may try to obligate that person through a get-rich-quick scheme or an attempt to entangle him into debt.

I've especially noticed that the devil goes to work when churches go into building programs. Every church I have done consulting work at that was going through a building program has had someone approach them with a scheme of so-called "blessing." I believe it is the same spirit that was behind the offer the King of Sodom made. Its aim was to distract Abraham from his true Source of supply.

Years ago, many rural churches had a what I call a "chicken dinner philosophy." When they needed extra finances, they would sell chicken dinners to raise money. Today, our "chicken dinners" are more sophisticated, but they are still a distraction from God's currency.

I faced a difficult decision once when we were building a facility to accommodate our youth and children's ministries. The congregation and I had set our hearts to build a state-of-the-art facility debt free. It was a big step for us.

One day, I was asking God for wisdom concerning this whole process. As I left my place of prayer, a gentleman called me on the phone, saying that he represented a company based in Tampa, Florida. He explained that the company had a small cruise ship docked in a port near us and they wanted to donate the ship to us as a tax write off. I immediately became excited and thought that this was an answer to my prayer. I scheduled a date for my team to survey the ship. But as I walked on board, the Holy Spirit dropped the word "trap" into my heart. Oh, I was grieved. What I thought was an answer to prayer was, in reality, a scheme of satan.

After that, I conducted a thorough investigation into the company that was making the offer. Their business was gambling. I realized that God would not use this to prosper us, and to the surprise of the company, I refused their offer.

Many people around me couldn't understand why I would turn against what appeared to be the provision of God. They questioned me with scripture taken out of context. "Doesn't the Bible say, 'The wealth of the wicked is laid up for the just'?"

But I couldn't disobey the Word that I had received in my heart. It was a trap.

I inquired of the Lord for wisdom concerning all of this and He told me that He wanted the people of the church to invest in the facility. He said that they needed "ownership" of the youth and children's ministries. I went to our congregation and challenged them to show their commitment and give generously.

God began to prosper our congregation for their willingness to give, and shortly thereafter, we were able to open our new facility debt free.

GOD HAS ALREADY BLESSED YOU

Did you know that you've already received the blessing of God?

> *God blessed them, and God said unto them, Be fruitful, and multiply….*
>
> *Genesis 1:28*

This is the very first statement that God spoke over mankind.

Think about it.

The very first statement He made was, *"Be blessed. Be fruitful. Multiply!"*

Yet, thousands of years later, we're still arguing whether or not God wants us to be blessed.

In the Christian community, it's a widespread belief that there is something wrong with individual success. Most Christians believe they should achieve only enough for their own material comfort and pass a little bit on to their children. This is a very narrow view of God—and honestly, it's stingy!

> *A good man leaveth an inheritance to his children's children….*
>
> *Proverbs 13:22*

The Bible teaches that a good man's life produces enough for multi-generational blessing.

That old, religious "subsistence" viewpoint is actually just false humility. It's birthed in the idea of scarcity—that by limiting oneself to "just enough," we will not be taking anything away from others who need what we have.

I cannot accept the idea that God, the Creator of the Universe, created a world where one person's gain must be another person's loss.

You were born blessed and you were born to be a blessing.

When you prosper to fulfill your purpose, it will not be so that you can simply consume better food, drive nicer cars, have multiple residences and wear beautiful clothing. Your life is much deeper than that. The world chases after those things. As a believer, those things will chase after you.

One day a minister friend of mine was showing me a fixed-up hot rod that he used to celebrate the actions of young people who distinguished themselves through a discipleship program he created. When I saw that car, I laughed out loud and said, *"I want a hot rod!"*

Within a couple of hours, my secretary called to inform me that someone drove a 1968 Corvette Stingray to the church and left the keys for me. They said, "The Lord wanted me to give this to Pastor Kennedy."

I was ecstatic and began to praise the Lord and laugh at his goodness toward me. Then I thought about the children's facility we were building. I called my secretary and instructed her to take a picture of the Corvette and sell it. I told her, we would invest the money in the children's ministry.

You know, I never have regretted that decision. I received my hot rod. I *didn't* have to drive it. I *didn't* have to park it in my garage. I had it and I could have kept it if I had wanted to, but I celebrated God's kindness and sold it to benefit our church.

I've determined in my life that I will always have things, but things will never have me.

> *I will make my covenant between me and thee,*
> *and will multiply thee exceedingly.*
> *Genesis 17:2*

Increase is within you. You must understand that you are already blessed by God to multiply. What you need to learn is how to open up the storehouse of God's currency and how to recognize His blessing when it comes.

Abraham experienced God's blessing. He understood that he was blessed to be a blessing.

> *...In thee shall all families of the earth be blessed.*
> *Genesis 12:3*

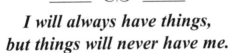

I will always have things,
but things will never have me.

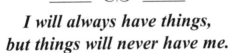

To firmly establish in your heart the Abrahamic concept of being blessed, you must "hear" from God that you are *personally* connected to His will to be blessed. Otherwise, you will sabotage your own success and limit yourself to a life of mediocrity.

Be open to receiving abundance right now. End the debate. Settle it with yourself once and for all that you are born for a purpose and God has blessed you so you can fulfill it.

Are you born to help fund world evangelism?

More than 3.6 million people accepted the invitation to accept Christ when Evangelist Reinhardt Bonnke preached in Lagos, Nigeria.

The campaign required money to fund it.

Are you created to drill water wells in Third World countries?

Water is the precious gift of life in many countries. Evangelists James and Betty Robison's *Life Outreach* drills water wells that literally save thousands of lives a day. Each well costs a mere $1,200!

The process of drilling wells requires money to fund it.

Are you appointed to rescue young girls from the modern-day slave trade?

Missionaries Doug and Ramona Jacobs' *Project Rescue* purchases young ladies from their pimps and grants them their freedom.

It requires money to fund it.

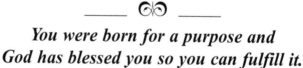

You were born for a purpose and
God has blessed you so you can fulfill it.

Are you called to help establish a church in a new city or growth area?

My second church plant required a $100,000 investment before we even held our first service. My friend, Evangelist Lynn Wheeler, plants churches in the Ukraine for $3,500 each!

Church planting requires money to fund it.

Are you burdened that children in Latin America live in city dumps and receive no education?

My friends, Missionaries Phil and Lori Schmidt, with *Latin American Child Care,* provide education, clothing and medical and dental care for over 80,000 children a day!

They require money to fund it.

Do you want the Bible to be printed in every language spoken upon the earth?

More than 270 million people still need the Bible translated into their language. Wycliffe Bible Translators (6,000 of them) are working diligently to reach all of them by the year 2025.

It requires money to fund it.

When the Iron Curtain fell and the former Soviet Union collapsed giving the opportunity to establish churches in Russia, Rick and Denise Renner from Tulsa, Oklahoma, left their comfort zone and moved to Riga, Latvia, to establish *The Good News Church.*

It requires money to fund it.

What about you?

What steps of faith are you now blessed to accomplish?

How can you take the blessings of God and become a blessing to mankind?

> *"...If anyone wants to be first, he must be the very last, and the servant of all."*
> **Mark 9:35 NIV**

Let's focus on putting ourselves into position as God's servants and receive His currency in order to truly become servants to this lost and dying the world.

THE RELEASE

൦⧸൦

YOUR ROLE IN RELEASING GOD'S BLESSINGS

6 GOD OPERATES THROUGH THE LAW OF EXCHANGE

Do you remember what currency is?

It is a medium of exchange.

How does God's currency work?

It works through the *Law of Exchange.* When you work with your hands, even if you don't know it, you are operating in the *Law of Exchange.* You are exchanging your time, talent, energy, intellect, ideas and influence for man's currency.

Now, stop reading and take a $20 bill out of your wallet and look at it for a minute.

How did you receive that particular $20 bill? What did you do to get it? Did you work an hour or more?

If you did, you exchanged your time for that $20.

Did you exchange a product for that $20?

Whatever the case, the person who released what he had in his hand (the $20 bill) for what you had in your hand (your time, talent, energy, intellect, ideas, product or influence) participated with you in the *Law of Exchange.*

The person who released the $20 bill believed that what was in your hand was **more valuable** to him than $20. Otherwise, he would not have made the exchange.

> *"It's no good, it's no good!" says the buyer; then off he goes and boasts about his purchase.*
> *Proverbs 20:14 NIV*

The *Law of Exchange* works as a method of commerce. It represents the exchange of values.

> *Without all contradiction the less is blessed of the better.*
> *Hebrews 7:7*

God uses the *Law of Exchange* to determine what you value most in life.

The tithe is also a currency of exchange. The tithe is the first part, the choice portion, the principal thing. The tithe represents and redeems the whole.

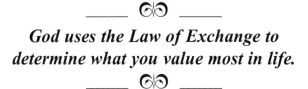

God uses the Law of Exchange to determine what you value most in life.

Only the first part redeems the whole. The second part does not qualify as the tithe. The second, third, forth, fifth, sixth, seventh, eighth, ninth, or tenth portion is merely a tip or gratuity. Only the *first* division of the ten qualifies as the tithe.

> *For where your treasure is, there will your heart be also.*
> *Matthew 6:21*

Tithing is a heart issue. The tithe represents your time, talent, energy, intellect or influence. The tithe represents the choice part of the whole of your life.

When you approach the Lord to worship Him with the tithe, in essence you are saying, *"God, this is the currency of man which represents the whole of my life—my time, my talent, my abilities, my influence and my worth. Remembering that you're the One who gives me the power to get wealth (Deuteronomy 8:18), I worship you with this tithe."*

Hearing that statement God, in essence, says to you, *"I will accept the tithe—man's currency—from you, representing your life; in exchange I offer you My blessing, representing My life."* God releases **the Word of His blessing** upon you when you tithe.

> **"Bring the whole tithe into the storehouse, that there may be food in my house. Test me in this,"** says the LORD Almighty, **"and see if I will not throw open the floodgates of heaven and pour out so much blessing that you will not have room enough for it."**
>
> *Malachi 3:10 NIV*

The religious mind doesn't think the thoughts of God. God's ways of operation are higher than ours (Isaiah 55:8). A common argument against the prosperity message is "It is wrong to give in order to get." Others use snippet jabs about our beliefs, like "name it, claim it," or "blab it, grab it."

But you cannot receive what you have not released.

Did God give His Son with the expectation to receive?

Does a farmer plant a field without expecting to harvest?

Does any worker refuse their paycheck?

Of course not. Most workers look at their checks and ask, "Is that all I get?" Solomon stated that no one is ever satisfied with his income (Ecclesiastes 5:10).

God operates by the same principles that He has ordained for man to use. He established the Law that states, "Thou shalt not murder." That tells us that God will not murder. His Law says, "Thou shalt not steal." God will not steal. Jesus proclaimed, *"The thief comes only to steal, kill, and to destroy"* (John 10:10). Yet, to hear some preachers talk, you wonder why they don't just come right out and accuse God of being a thief.

Just like any other law in the Bible, God has established the *Law of Exchange.* It works through giving *and* receiving.

> *For God so loved the world, that he gave his only begotten Son, that whosoever believeth in him should not perish, but have everlasting life.*
> *John 3:16*

> *I tell you the truth, unless a kernel of wheat falls to the ground and dies, it remains only a single seed. But if it dies, it produces many seeds.*
> *John 12:24 NIV*

God practiced the Law of Exchange in order to receive us.

When the world was thrust into poverty, sin and death because of man's willful disobedience, God sowed the Seed into the earth that would create a new harvest of sons.

God practiced the *Law of Exchange* **in order to receive us.** He released His Son in order to receive sons.

> *Remember this: Whoever sows sparingly will also reap sparingly, and whoever sows generously will also reap generously. Each man should give what he has decided in his heart to give, not reluctantly or under compulsion, for God loves a cheerful*

giver.

II Corinthians 9:6-7 NIV

He that spared not his own Son, but delivered him up for us all, how shall he not with him also freely give us all things?

Romans 8:32

If God was willing to give His Son for us, He is not withholding any other good things from us.

For where your treasure is, there will your heart be also.

Matthew 6:21

Looking where He invested His treasure reveals God's heart. He invested His treasure in you!

7 SEED OFFERINGS: THE KEY TO MULTIPLICATION

While the earth remaineth, seedtime and harvest, and cold and heat, and summer and winter, and day and night shall not cease.

Genesis 8:22

If you want to multiply your resources, you must understand the principle of seed.

A few years back, I took an evangelist friend golfing. While we were on the golf course we began to talk about the Word of God. I shared how my wife and I had sowed a seed offering for the purpose of receiving a new house. Then I testified how God had blessed us with our dream home.

I noticed a puzzled look on his face. "Neil, explain to me what you mean by the term *seed offering,*" he said.

I couldn't believe it. This evangelist had been in the ministry longer than I had been saved and he had never heard of a seed offering. I suggested that we forgo the rest of the game and have lunch. I'll never forget sitting down in the courtyard of the golf course, opening up the Word and explaining God's supernatural principle of *Seedtime and Harvest* to my dear friend.

Up until then, my friend had faithfully served God, ministering in churches all over the United States. He struggled for fifteen years to stay on the road serving as an evangelist.

That day he began to practice planting seeds to multiply his ministry. Today his ministry has never been larger and has even financed the planting of several churches in the Ukraine.

Give according to your heart's capacity.

What can you truly believe God for? What is your capacity?

> *He which soweth sparingly shall reap also sparingly; and he which soweth bountifully shall reap also bountifully. Every man according as he purposeth in his heart, [so let him give]; not grudgingly, or of necessity: for God loveth a cheerful giver.*
>
> *II Corinthians 9:6-7*

Do you realize that you determine your capacity for blessing? Paul taught that every man decides his own harvest.

What can you truly believe God for?

The capacity of your heart determines your future. Your reaping is in direct proportion to your sowing. If you sow reluctantly, you will have a minimal harvest. If you are generous, you will have an abundant harvest.

Sounds simple doesn't it?

It is simple—however, few people truly live according to this principle.

Be not deceived; God is not mocked: for
whatsoever a man soweth, that shall he also reap.
Galatians 6:7

The *type* and the *quantity* of harvest you receive are
determined by your decisions.

Let me be honest. Few people appreciate what I am about
to say. In fact, many people become very upset with this
statement, but it's true nonetheless. Most people are
looking for an excuse—an explanation for life's troubles—
other than the real truth.

In my book, *The Seven Laws Which Govern Divine
Increase And Order,* I explained the *Law of Seed.* Believers
are creationists, not evolutionists. Our lives are the
products of the seed we have planted.

Isaac is a Biblical example of a man who understood how
to sow seed for an abundant harvest.

Isaac planted crops in that land and the same year
reaped a hundredfold, because the LORD blessed
him. The man became rich, and his wealth
continued to grow until he became very wealthy.
Genesis 26:12-13 NIV

A famine had devastated the region. Most people at that
time had moved to Egypt where the economy was
flourishing. But the Lord had appeared to Isaac and said,
"Do not go down to Egypt; live in the land where I tell
you to live...I will bless you" (Genesis 26:2).

With the blessing of the Lord, Isaac planted crops in a land
of famine and reaped a hundredfold!

He that tilleth his land shall be satisfied with
bread: but he that followeth vain persons is void
of understanding.
Proverbs 12:11

Isaac didn't follow the crowd. He was led by the Word of Lord.

If you're going to prosper, there will be times that you must refuse the so-called "wisdom" of the day. **Even when the economy is suffering, it is always a good time to plant seeds.**

Many people have the opposite strategy during times of lack. They hide, hoard and succumb to the pressure of fear rather than trust the principle of *Seedtime and Harvest.*

In my ministry I have faced many times of financial pressure. Each time has come as a result of stepping out to do what God called me to do. You would think that if God called you to do something, everything would go smoothly—that it would be easy. Yet, it seems to be the opposite. Sometimes it seems as if all Hell breaks out against you.

That's when it's time to trust in the principles God has established. He established the principle of planting seed in order to ensure a harvest. **Seed is the key to multiplication.**

> *So let him give; not grudgingly, or of necessity:*
> *for God loveth a cheerful giver.*
> *II Corinthians 9:7*

My giving to God cannot operate the principles of Scripture unless I give with integrity. Many people fail to receive a harvest from their giving because they give reluctantly or under compulsion.

To give *reluctantly* means *"to give out of annoyance, pain or grief."*

I served as a consultant for a church facing a large relocation. We interviewed a financial group we were considering to help us complete the task. One of the representatives of the organization laughingly described the capital-raising programs that his church had just completed saying, "I've been *the victim* of two campaigns now."

That man won't see a reward for his giving with that attitude. In fact, after we heard that comment, we withdrew from his company as a potential financial resource for us. That one comment cost him multiple thousands of dollars!

We are not to give out of compulsion.

Compulsive giving means that you are *"imposed upon to give or required to give by legal obligation."*

Most churches, ministries and Christian organizations place a requirement on people to give. They make giving out to be a legal obligation. The result of this emphasis is a failed system of financing the kingdom.

_____ ൬ _____

The only time that Law is required is when the heart is absent.

_____ ൬ _____

The Old Testament is filled with legal obligations to give this and that. In the New Testament, giving is placed on a higher order.

The only time that Law is required is when the heart is absent.

Let me explain that statement.

Our courtrooms are filled with fathers receiving judgments and court orders to pay child support to their children—*to their own children!* It's sad to say, but it requires the law to get these deadbeat fathers to do what is right. It should be a burning desire in their hearts to take care of their children. **The Law is required when the heart is absent.**

The same principle is true for the Christian. It should not require the Law to compel us to do what is right! It should be on our hearts to give whatever we can whenever we can.

Do not despise small seeds.

My wife, Kay, and I have made it a habit to walk each morning when I am at home. One day we were walking briskly when she stopped suddenly. *(I thought she was faking a "tie your shoe" breather.)* She lifted her hand into the air and proclaimed, "Do not despise small beginnings!" She had found a penny.

I said, "That's cute. Let's go."

The next day, we were walking again. Sure enough, she stopped, bent over, picked up another penny and proclaimed, "Do not despise small beginnings!"

Again I said, "That's cute. Now, let's go."

The following day it was the same thing, but this time Kay had found a dime.

By this point I was taking notice.

A few days later, we were walking when Kay yelled out suddenly. I thought that she might have seen a lizard or a snake. She ran over to the curb, picked something up and unfolded a ten-dollar bill! She lifted it up and proclaimed, "DO NOT DESPISE SMALL BEGINNINGS!"

You ought to see how I walk now. I'm sure I look goofy as I go along looking around at the ground. But I'm happy to report that I found my first penny just a few days later.

Not too long after that, Kay and I were walking along when I excitedly ran toward a shining penny. When I reached down to pick it up I called for Kay to help me. Our walk was interrupted that day because we found 236 pennies and nickels.

I learned a very important principle from this process.

God did not pour out those pennies from Heaven. People dropped them. Some man released them out of his hand and despised small beginnings so much that he wouldn't even bend over and pick them up.

Some man repelled what he disrespected.

On the flip side, Kay and I attracted what we respected.

It is estimated that over one billion dollars worth of U.S. currency is currently sitting in fountains, in coin jars or is simply lost somewhere.

Do not depise small seeds.

Gather the fragments.

Our attitude should be like that of Christ Jesus when he received a boy's lunch *(another small beginning)*.

> *Andrew, Simon Peter's brother, spoke up, "Here is a boy with five small barley loaves and two small fish, but how far will they go among so many?" Jesus said, "Have the people sit down." There was plenty of grass in that place, and the men sat down, about five thousand of them. Jesus then took the loaves, gave thanks, and distributed to those who were seated as much as they wanted. He did the same with the fish. When they had all had enough to eat, he said to his disciples, "Gather the pieces that are left over. Let nothing be wasted." So they gathered them and filled twelve baskets with the pieces of the five barley loaves left over by those who had eaten.*
> *John 6:8-13 NIV*

Jesus said, *"Gather the pieces that are left over. Let nothing be wasted."*

Some people have the idea that since Jesus could multiply five loaves and two fish to feed the multitude, He wouldn't care about the fragments. But nothing could be more wrong. Jesus believes in good stewardship. He is careful about the little things.

I have consulted with pastors and their staff members in small, growing churches who were very careful about minding all the little details, but when their churches became large those ministers changed their attitudes. As their congregations grew, those pastors began to treat small things with contempt. When that happens, it's usually not too long before they find themselves in a financial crunch. Their attitude permeates the organization, and people begin to hold on to their small offerings because they see that they are not respected.

> *When you have eaten and are satisfied, praise the LORD your God for the good land he has given you. Be careful that you do not forget the LORD your God, failing to observe his commands, his laws and his decrees that I am giving you this day. Otherwise, when you eat and are satisfied, when you build fine houses and settle down, and when your herds and flocks grow large and your silver and gold increase and all you have is multiplied, then your heart will become proud and you will forget the LORD your God.*
>
> *Deuteronomy 8:10-14 NIV*

A key to multiplication is to be thankful and faithful in little things. Pride causes a person, or an organization, to develop a disdain toward smallness. It's the little things that make or break you.

Anytime I feel like I'm loosing ground financially, I check my attitude toward small things—am I being faithful in the little things?

> *Dishonest money dwindles away, but he who*
> *gathers money little by little makes it grow.*
> *Proverbs 13:11 NIV*

8 THE PRINCIPAL THING

...And Abel was a keeper of sheep, but Cain was a tiller of the ground. And in process of time it came to pass, that Cain brought of the fruit of the ground an offering unto the LORD. And Abel, he also brought of the firstlings of his flock and of the fat thereof. And the LORD had respect unto Abel and to his offering: But unto Cain and to his offering he had not respect. And Cain was very wroth, and his countenance fell.

Genesis 4:2-5

This is the very first record of an offering given unto the Lord. Both Cain and Abel participated in this offering, however, only Abel's offering was received with respect. God did not look at Cain's offering with respect.

Cain brought some of the fruits. Abel brought fat portions from the firstborn.

Cain's offering was the equivalent of a tip. The Lord was not honored by Cain's giving. Cain's gift was a mere token of his income.

Abel's offering was the best portion of the firstborn. His gift represented the principal thing he owned. His gift was a tithe.

The principal thing is the first, the beginning, the chief part or the choice portion. The principal thing redeems the whole.

Cain's offering wasn't received because it wasn't a reflection of gratitude or joy. He gave out of a motive of obligation. Cain felt compelled to give, but he did not honor God.

When Cain found out that his offering was disrespected, he became very angry.

> *Then the LORD said to Cain, "Why are you angry? Why is your face downcast? If you do what is right, will you not be accepted? But if you do not do what is right, sin is crouching at your door; it desires to have you, but you must master it."*
>
> *Genesis 4:6-7 NIV*

The Lord attempted to correct Cain's attitude toward the offering. It was within Cain's ability to do what was right. He chose not to. Cain decided in his heart that God was not deserving of true worship. Cain's attitude was reflected in his actions. The result was devastating—anger, depression, bitterness, isolation and a spirit of competition consumed him.

Rather than repent and change his way of doing things, Cain invited his brother to go on a walk into the field.

> *Now Cain said to his brother Abel, "Let's go out to the field." And while they were in the field, Cain attacked his brother Abel and killed him.*
>
> *Genesis 4:8 NIV*

The first murder ever committed was over an offering to the Lord!

In my years of ministry, I've never preached a message on tithes, offerings or on prosperity where I didn't face a spirit of violent opposition.

_____ ෨ _____

The first murder ever committed was over an offering to the Lord!

_____ ෨ _____

If you listen to a teaching concerning giving unto the Lord and, rather than feeling joy, you become angry, you are accepting the spirit of Cain. You are allowing a murderous spirit to attempt to control you!

> *By faith Abel offered God a better sacrifice than Cain did. By faith he was commended as a righteous man, when God spoke well of his offerings. And by faith he still speaks, even though he is dead.*
> *Hebrews 11:4 NIV*

Abel is recorded as the first hero of faith in the eleventh chapter of Hebrews. He is the man who redeemed himself out of poverty by practicing the tithe.

By acting in faith, Abel called those things that are not as though they were. Abel approached God, believing that He existed and that He would reward those who diligently sought Him (Hebrews 11:6).

> *Honour the LORD with thy substance, and with the firstfruits of all thine increase: So shall thy barns be filled with plenty, and thy presses shall burst out with new wine.*
> *Proverbs 3:9-10*

I practiced tithing for years before I realized that I was not actually giving *the tithe.* I received income and held onto it for days, or even weeks, before I would write the check. It was simply a sloppy habit. My paying the tithe became like paying the fire-insurance, the electric bill, or whatever, but it wasn't an act of my worship.

The tithe is the principal thing, the firstfruits, the choice part and the chief portion. In scripture, it is the tithe that redeems the whole and buys it back for use.

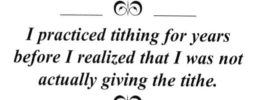

I practiced tithing for years before I realized that I was not actually giving the tithe.

As I was meditating on this principle, the Holy Spirit spoke to me saying, *"Neil, the tithe represents what is most important in your life."* He went on to explain the tithe this way:

- If I pay the mortgage payment before I worship God with the tithe, I declare that my house is my temple.

- If I pay the car payment with the tithe, I declare that my car is an image to be worshipped. (Haven't we all known people who are delusional enough to think that they *are* what they drive?)

- If I buy groceries before I pay my tithe, I declare that my stomach is my god. (The reason many people have bloated stomachs and digestive issues is because they *eat* their tithe.)

- If I spend the tithe on clothes or things for myself, I have declared myself a god.

    …Many live as enemies of the cross of Christ. Their destiny is destruction, their god is their stomach, and their glory is in their shame. Their

mind is on earthly things.
Philippians 3:18-19

After hearing from the Lord, I carefully examined my attitude and knowledge concerning the tithe. After exhaustive study and prayer, Kay and I began to *truly worship* the Lord with the firstfruits of our income.

The process and principles of our worshiping the Lord with the tithe are simple. We practice them every time.

1. First, we recognize that the tithe is the *first part* of all our income. We pay it before we pay anything else.

2. Next, we lift our tithe check before the Lord, waving it and declaring our thanksgiving to Him. We thank God with a heart of gratitude and respect for Him and declare that it is God who gives us the ability to produce.

3. Then, we speak over our tithe. We say, "This, the tithe, represents and redeems the whole of our income."

4. Finally, we share communion together and worship the Lord.

I can't express the emotions that are released when you are obedient to worship the Lord with the tithe. A sense of security envelopes you. When I worship God with my tithe, I feel a sense of destiny.

In the New International Version, Proverbs 3:9 says, *"Your barns will be filled to overflowing."*

That sounds great doesn't it?

The word for *barn* is the same as *"storehouse."* Just as God has storehouses of bounty, we are to have storehouses filled to overflowing.

How would you like to have your banker call and suggest that you open up new accounts because your accounts are too full to be covered by their insurance?

That's what it means to be filled to overflowing.

David R. Williams points out in his book entitled, *The Road To Radical Riches,* (Lansing, MI: Decapolis Publishing, 2000), that the word *filled*, in Proverbs 3:9, is the Hebrew word *"mala,"* which has a three-fold meaning:

1. It means *"to draw."* The picture is that God Himself *will draw* wealth to your storehouses.

2. It means *"to flow."* Wealth *will flow* to your storehouses in a steady stream.

3. It also means *"to replenish."* Whatever you give out *will be replenished, restocked and restored.*

> **The LORD shall command the blessing upon thee in thy storehouses, and in all that thou settest thine hand unto; and he shall bless thee in the land which the LORD thy God giveth thee.**
> **Deuteronomy 28:8**

I can't imagine anyone having an issue with tithing! It's the only practice in which God challenges us to put Him to the test.

> **"Test me in this," says the LORD Almighty, "and see if I will not throw open the floodgates of heaven and pour out so much blessing that you will not have room enough for it."**
> **Malachi 3:10 NIV**

Do you think that God could fail this test?

Do you think that God would lie?

God emphatically **guarantees** that He will throw open the floodgates of Heaven and pour out His blessing!

What is His blessing?

How will you recognize it when Heaven is opened up to you?

You must learn how to recognize the currencies of God.

THE EXCHANGE

∞

GOD'S CURRENCY
IN YOUR LIFE

9 GOD'S CURRENCY: WISDOM

The LORD has blessed my master abundantly, and he has become wealthy. He has given him sheep and cattle, silver and gold, menservants and maidservants, and camels and donkeys.
Genesis 24:34 NIV

Abraham was made abundantly wealthy by God through multiple streams of income. Abraham's streams of income included eight different avenues.

There is great wisdom in this, as we'll see in more detail later in this book. But if you're going to have great wealth, you must learn to master abundance.

God gives multiple streams of blessing to His children (Malachi 3:10).

Wisdom is the principal thing.
Proverbs 4:7

When you tithe, the first storehouse of bounty opened to you is wisdom. Wisdom is a currency of God.

For the LORD giveth wisdom.
Proverbs 2:6

God is generous with wisdom to anyone who requests it.

> *If any of you lacks wisdom, he should ask God,*
> *who gives generously to all without finding fault,*
> *and it will be given to him.*
>
> *James 1:5 NIV*

The currency of God's wisdom is greater than money.

Remember the old proverb that says, *"If you give a person a fish you feed him today, but if you teach a person to fish you feed him for a lifetime."* If you have wisdom, you will have a lifetime of provision. Money is fleeting, but wisdom is eternal.

When given the choice, always choose wisdom over money.

> *For wisdom is better than rubies; and all the*
> *things that may be desired are not to be compared*
> *to it.*
>
> *Proverbs 8:11*

Solomon is an example of a man who valued the wisdom of God more than money.

When you tithe, the first storehouse of bounty opened to you is wisdom.

Solomon was the second child of King David and Bathsheba. He inherited the kingdom of Israel directly from his father while his brother Adonijah attempted a coup d'état. Without the intervention of wisdom, Solomon would have never held on to his destiny as king.

After Solomon firmly established himself over his kingdom, he went up to the bronze altar at Gibeon to worship the Lord. Solomon offered the Lord a sacrifice of 1,000 burnt offerings. *(That may sound like a lot, but remember that in order for a sacrifice to be acceptable, it must be significant to the giver.)*

After the worship service, the Lord visited Solomon in the night.

> *"...Ask for whatever you want me to give you."*
> *II Chronicles 1:7 NIV*

A thousand things could run through your mind. Think about it.

What would you say? What would you ask for?

Solomon focused on the great currency of God—wisdom.

> *"Give me wisdom and knowledge...."*
> *II Chronicles 1:10 NIV*

God responded.

> *"...Since this is your heart's desire and you have not asked for wealth, riches or honor, nor for the death of your enemies, and since you have not asked for a long life but for wisdom and knowledge...wisdom and knowledge will be given to you. I will also give you wealth, riches and honor, such as no king who was before you ever had and none after you will have."*
> *II Chronicles 1:11-12 NIV*

Wisdom is the principal thing. When you receive the currency of wisdom from God's storehouse, everything you didn't ask for becomes yours as a by-product.

Solomon did not ask for wealth. His priority as king was the kingdom.

> *How much better to get wisdom than gold, to choose understanding rather than silver!*
> *Proverbs 16:16 NIV*

When you receive God's currency of wisdom, people will seek you out to exchange the currency of men for what you have. The Queen of Sheba was drawn to Solomon because of his wisdom. She transferred enormous wealth to him for the opportunity to share in what God had given to him.

> *She said to the king, "The report I heard in my own country about your achievements and your wisdom is true. But I did not believe these things until I came and saw with my own eyes. Indeed, not even half was told me; in wisdom and wealth you have far exceeded the report I heard. How happy your men must be! How happy your officials, who continually stand before you and hear your wisdom! Praise be to the LORD your God, who has delighted in you and placed you on the throne of Israel. Because of the LORD's eternal love for Israel, he has made you king, to maintain justice and righteousness." And she gave the king 120 talents of gold, large quantities of spices, and precious stones. Never again were so many spices brought in as those the queen of Sheba gave to King Solomon.*
>
> *I Kings 10:6-10 NIV*

The transfer of wealth comes by the exchange of God's currency through you. Men exchange their currency for what is unavailable to them otherwise.

The transfer of wealth comes by the exchange of God's currency through you.

> *To the man who pleases him, God gives wisdom, knowledge and happiness, but to the sinner he gives the task of gathering and storing up wealth to hand it over to the one who pleases God....*
>
> *Ecclesiastes 2:26 NIV*

Not only did Solomon gain wealth as a by-product of wisdom but he also gained protection from his enemies.

> ***Do not forsake wisdom, and she will protect you.***
> ***Proverbs 4:8***

No king could arise against Solomon because of his wisdom. While other kings paid their adversaries off or went to war, foreign kings paid Solomon for his alliance.

Wisdom is the application of John 10:10—life more abundantly.

When you worship God with the tithe, the storehouse of His bounty is open to you and the first, the beginning, the chief part, the choice portion and the principal thing—God's wisdom flows into your life.

10 GOD'S CURRENCY: KNOWLEDGE & SKILL

...God gave them knowledge and skill in all learning and wisdom....

Daniel 1:17

Daniel was exiled to Babylon (modern-day Iraq). While there, he prospered greatly because God favored him with wisdom, knowledge and skill in learning.

Knowledge is perception. It's the ability to see, understand, comprehend and retain. It literally means *"to make discovery."*

God has provided the currency of knowledge for you.

...No eye has seen, no ear has heard, no mind has conceived what God has prepared for those who love him—but God has revealed it to us by his Spirit....

I Corinthians 2:9-10 NIV

God is not keeping secrets *from* you; He is keeping secrets *for* you.

Daniel's knowledge surpassed that of his peers ten-fold (Daniel 1:20).

Daniel was elevated to a high position in a foreign government because of his knowledge (Daniel 2:48).

Do you see a man skilled in his work? He will
serve before kings; he will not serve before
obscure men.

Proverbs 22:29

God gives you knowledge to solve a problem that
otherwise is unanswered. And within each unanswered
problem is a key to abundance.

One day while working as a traveling salesman to support
his family, a man named King C. Gillette cut himself
shaving. In his day, razors needed continual sharpening.
Because of their design, they became worn out quickly. As
the blade became dull, replacement of the entire razor was
necessary, making them very expensive. But Gillette hit
upon an idea. He realized that a profit could be made by
selling a safety razor at a reduced price and then making
available inexpensive, disposable replacement blades to fit
it. Gillette developed a replaceable blade made out of very
thin sheet-steel. Once a razor blade became dull, it could
be discarded and replaced by a new sharp one, using the
same holder.

Is there abundance in a small idea?

In 2005, Procter & Gamble Company paid 57 billion dollars
for the Gillette Company!

If the ax is dull and its edge unsharpened, more
strength is needed, but skill will bring success.
Ecclesiastes 10:10 NIV

There are three keys in learning how to exercise knowledge
so that skill can bring you success:

1. Believe that God already has a plan awaiting your
   discovery.

2. Realize that God will give to those who ask of Him.

3. Understand that the plan requires obedience, discipline and implementation.

> *If you fully obey the LORD your God and carefully follow all his commands I give you today, the LORD your God will set you high above all the nations on earth.*
>
> *Deuteronomy 28:1 NIV*

A few months ago, my wife and I were on a trip. We had just received the very disturbing news that Kay's mother had been diagnosed with a brain tumor. While driving, we began to talk about the goodness of God and His desire for people to be healed and to live in divine health.

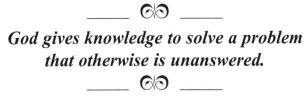

God gives knowledge to solve a problem that otherwise is unanswered.

Suddenly Kay turned to me and said, "Neil, I've got an idea! Let's design a beautiful pillow with the word 'HEALTH' embroidered on the front of it. And let's write a book that teaches God's will for health and healing and include scriptures for people to use as confessions of faith. I can design a hidden pocket in the back of the pillow for the book—just the way you hide the Word of God in your heart."

Wanting to support her mother both in prayer and in a tangible way, Kay immediately went to work crafting the first *Pillow of Promise* while I prayerfully wrote the book. In no time at all, we presented our gift to my mother-in-law, commissioning it with prayer as a point of contact for our faith. Daily, my mother-in-law would rest her head upon the pillow and confess the scriptures for her healing. Today, we are overjoyed to announce that Kay's mother has received a clean bill of health!

Since then, hundreds of *Pillows of Promise* have been delivered to people facing the challenges of sickness and disease. We receive testimonies each week of God's grace, and we have been able to use a simple, every-day article made of cloth for His glory.

"A pillow is to the head what a promise is to the heart."
— Neil Kennedy —

Of course my wife is expanding the *Pillows of Promise* line to include other promises from God.

The call of God upon Kay to minister healing was dormant until she received God's currency of knowledge to release her skill.

How can your skills be used to bring glory to God?

Believe Him for knowledge to open up new realms of possibility where you can faithfully apply your talents to His purposes.

11 GOD'S CURRENCY: FAVOR & INFLUENCE

A good name is rather to be chosen than great riches, and loving favor rather than silver and gold.

Proverbs 22:1

The Persian King Xerxes wanted to replace his unfaithful wife Vashti with someone more suitable to be his queen. The king's counselors advised him to hold a beauty pageant in order to find the best candidate to become his next wife.

Esther was an orphaned Jewish girl, who had been brought up by her cousin Mordecai to be entered in the contest. Esther was taken to the king's palace and entrusted to Hegai, a eunuch who was in charge of the royal harem.

> *The girl pleased him and won his favor. Immediately he provided her with her beauty treatments and special food. He assigned to her seven maids selected from the king's palace and moved her and her maids into the best place in the harem.*
>
> *Esther 2:9 NIV*

Favor positioned Esther to receive what money could not buy. Esther was immediately set apart from her peers in the best place in the harem. Hegai began a series of beauty treatments and a special diet for her. Favor even afforded seven maids to attend to her needs.

Favor will promote you above your peers.

Favor is a currency of God that flows into your life to put you into special positions of influence.

> *Before a girl's turn came to go in to King Xerxes, she had to complete twelve months of beauty treatments prescribed for the women, six months with oil of myrrh and six with perfumes and cosmetics.*
>
> *Esther 2:12 NIV*

Imagine. The protocol of approaching the king required twelve months of preparation! And when the time came, Esther was prepared.

> *Now the king was attracted to Esther more than to any of the other women, and she won his favor and approval….*
>
> *Esther 2:17 NIV*

Esther received the royal crown and became the new queen. The king gave a great banquet in her honor, distributing gifts generously throughout Persia.

Favor prospers you.

Within one year's time, favor moved Esther from poverty to the palace.

Favor is divine influence emanating on your behalf. Favor produces results in your life without apparent force. It is the invisible quality of attraction.

> *…You have come to royal position for such a time as this.*
>
> *Esther 4:14 NIV*

Esther was put into a position of influence for a reason.

God promotes and prospers people on purpose.

An anti-Christ spirit in the person of Haman wielded his influence to attempt to kill all of the Jews in Persia. *(This spirit arises often. There have been many attempts to obliterate the Jewish people.)* Satan hates the people of God, but God's favor acted on their behalf, even before they knew that they would need it.

As a born-again child of God, God's currency of favor works on your behalf. It goes before you. It prepares you for future invents.

_____ ᎙ _____

Favor flows into your life to put you into special positions of influence.

᎙

A few years ago, I preached on the topic of favor at Calvary Assembly of God in Decatur, Alabama. We had a wonderful service with many people responding to receive the favor of God upon their lives, families and businesses. Pastor George Sawyer told me after the service that he had never preached on the subject of God's favor before and that he planned to begin a series on the subject.

As he prepared to preach on favor a few Sundays later, the Holy Spirit prompted Pastor Sawyer to wait one week before he began the series. Over the course of that next week, and before he preached his first sermon on the topic, a couple asked for an appointment to see him. During the meeting the couple said, "Pastor, we know that you have something big on your heart for Calvary Assembly, and God has shown us favor. We want to sow this into the ministry for your dream." They then handed him a stock transfer order valued at over one million dollars.

They didn't know what the dream was that Pastor Sawyer had on his heart. But God did. God released favor into the lives of this couple so they could share that favor with the church.

> *"The Spirit of the Lord is on me, because he has anointed me to preach good news to the poor. He has sent me to proclaim freedom for the prisoners and recovery of sight for the blind, to release the oppressed, to proclaim the year of the Lord's favor."*
>
> *Luke 4:18-19 NIV*

Jesus declared that His coming ushered in the time of God's favor. God's currency of favor is a spiritual force that goes before you seemingly unnoticed. It will promote you, prosper you, position you and bring about what God has purposed for you.

12 GOD'S CURRENCY: REVELATION & DISCERNMENT

I will praise the LORD, who counsels me; even at night my heart instructs me.

Psalm 16:7 NIV

Surely the Lord GOD will do nothing, but he revealeth his secret unto his servants the prophets.

Amos 3:7

The Bible teaches that God will do nothing without revealing His secrets to His prophets beforehand.

Why would God limit Himself to that?

So that His prophets would do what prophets do—namely, prophesy. In other words, God reveals His will to the prophets so that they will foretell what God is going to do.

Revelation means *"divine vision with respect to future events."*

And Joseph dreamed a dream….

Genesis 37:5

Joseph was a young man when he received revelation from God in his dreams. Joseph's dreams foretold of future events and his life became a revelation to the world of the coming Messiah, Jesus.

Some people envy dreamers. **Those who don't dream despise those who do.**

Have you ever had people ridicule your dreams?

Truthfully, few people rejoice over other people's dreams. It's a sad fact that it's often the people closest to you that hate you the most when you dream. Your own family members may rebuke you just as Joseph's did (Genesis 37:10).

Naively Joseph shared his dream prematurely with his brothers. They hated Joseph. They despised him for his dream and plotted to kill him. Ungodly men may even take on a murderous spirit against you because of the revelation that you have been given by God (Genesis 37:19-20)

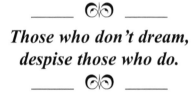

Those who don't dream,
despise those who do.

Read this carefully: **When you receive revelation from God, satan will come immediately to attack your dream in its infancy.** The devil's purpose is to abort your future.

> *Satan cometh immediately, and taketh away the word that was sown in their hearts.*
>
> *Mark 4:15*

When Moses was born, the spirit of abortion moved Pharaoh to kill the children of Israel. When Jesus was born, the same spirit of abortion moved King Herod to slay the infants. Both Pharaoh and Herod feared the revelation of God's Word even though it was only in its beginnings.

Joseph survived the attempt on his life; yet he was sold into slavery.

When you have a revelation from God, others will attempt to enslave your dream. If the enemy can trap you into a job or a career that is outside of God's plan, he may keep you from achieving your destiny. If the enemy can bind you with debt, you will forfeit the resources you need to accomplish your dream.

My daughter is attending Southeastern University in Lakeland, Florida. When she shared with me her desire to receive her education to fulfill the call of God upon her life, I was thrilled. But, I told her, "Alex, I will not allow you to become a slave to a lender. We will believe God for the provision. We won't borrow a dime to pay for your education. You will graduate owing no one a debt except the continued debt of love. Then you'll be free to fulfill your destiny."

I just can't agree with the process of receiving an education, yet owing thousands of dollars upon graduation. This kind of debt is keeping young people from fulfilling their God-given assignments in life. As God provides for Alex's education, she'll be free to step into her assignment without the burden of debt. *(Now if I can make sure she marries someone with the same philosophy...)*

God's currency is revelation. God will give you insight for your future.

> *"For I know the plans I have for you," declares*
> *the LORD, "plans to prosper you and not to harm*
> *you, plans to give you hope and a future."*
> *Jeremiah 29:11 NIV*

I can't tell you how amazing it is to know that God has a secret for you. He is holding on to that secret, waiting to reveal it to you upon your request. I often awaken in the night to spend time with God's Spirit and He reveals His purposes to me.

> *A man's heart deviseth his way: but the LORD*
> *directeth his steps.*
>
> *Proverbs 16:9*

Joseph's journey from being thrown into the pit to being given the second highest position in all of Egypt was not an easy one; however, God directed his steps to succeed. Because Joseph was filled with revelation and discernment he was given a place of honor. The blessing of God made a place for him.

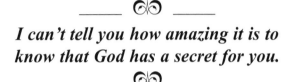

I can't tell you how amazing it is to
know that God has a secret for you.

> *A gift opens the way for the giver and ushers him*
> *into the presence of the great.*
>
> *Proverbs 18:16 NIV*

Joseph secured the economy of Egypt because he had a revelation of the seven good years to come. He even prospered during the famine through an ingenious economic strategy. He established business systems of management that wise governments and corporations still use today.

Through his discernment Joseph saved countless lives and preserved the Jewish race.

God's currency of revelation and discernment will secure you and your family for the future.

One day the Spirit of the Lord gave me insight that I would receive a call within two weeks time inviting me to move to a new place in ministry. I shared with my wife what I had heard from the Lord, and sure enough, two weeks later I received the phone call. Without having prior revelation from the Lord, I would not have made the move.

Even though I was excited about the move, Kay was still troubled in her mind. Then she began to pray for clarity. As we were traveling to visit our new location before we actually moved, the Spirit of the Lord spoke to Kay asking her, "Can you spend two years to invest in Neil's family?" (The move was going to place us near some of my relatives.)

When Kay realized the Lord had a special plan for this change in our lives, she answered Him with a resounding, "Yes."

The next two years were eventful. I was able to share Christ with my 89-year-old grandfather, leading him to the saving knowledge of the Lord. I had the joy of praying the sinner's prayer with him. Not long after that, he passed away.

When you receive God's currency of revelation and discernment, you are able to take steps toward future events with confidence knowing that God is leading you into your divine destiny.

13 GOD'S CURRENCY: CREATIVITY, IDEAS & INVENTIONS

And Uzziah prepared for them throughout all the host shields, and spears, and helmets, and habergeons, and bows, and slings to cast stones. And he made in Jerusalem engines, invented by cunning men, to be on the towers and upon the bulwarks, to shoot arrows and great stones withal. And his name spread far abroad; for he was marvelously helped, till he was strong.
II Chronicles 26:14-15

Uzziah was only sixteen years old when he became king. He was known to seek the Lord and to do what was right. The Prophet Zachariah tutored him. Uzziah enjoyed great success in all that he did. He invented engines, devices used for military defense. He learned to use equipment to overcome a strong force of opposition. Because of his creativity and resourcefulness, his fame spread across the nations, causing his enemies to fear him.

Just as it was to Uzziah, **God's currency of creativity is available to us.** He is the Supreme Creator and we are created in His image and likeness.

Early on in the scriptures, we also read of a man named Jubal who invented the first musical instruments (Genesis 4:21). Jubal is recorded as the first person who gave man the ability to express musical praise from his heart. *(This is now a multi-billion dollar industry.)*

When I pioneered my second church in Orlando, Florida, I asked a man to join my team as Worship Pastor. This man had a distinguished career with an award-winning contemporary Christian musical group. He continued to travel with the group while leading our new congregation in worship on the weekends.

During one service, I prophesied over this man that he would begin to hear new songs in his spirit to write. Within a just few months, he wrote dozens of new worship songs. Our congregation was blessed immensely because of his creativity. Some of those songs have since become number-one hit singles and were released on his first solo project. He now leads worship in one of America's largest churches.

> *I wisdom dwell with prudence, and find out knowledge of witty inventions.*
> *Proverbs 8:12*

I like the way Dr. Mike Murdock puts it. He says, "One idea from God can make you an income for the rest of your life."

I quoted that statement during a sermon one day and a woman picked up on what I said. A few weeks later she approached me for prayer. She said that she was traveling to New York City the next day to meet with a major designer. I inquired as to what the meeting was pertaining. She told me, "I invented a special stitch that the designer wants to lease from me for $10,000 a month."

WOW! *(I didn't even know that you could lease a stitch!)*

> *The purposes of a man's heart are deep waters, but a man of understanding draws them out.*
> *Proverbs 20:5 NIV*

Deep within you, God has deposited purposes that can only be drawn out through understanding.

I visited a small church in Florida with a giant vision a few months ago. While I was there, I spoke on the topic of God's currency, and I specifically talked about creativity, ideas and witty inventions. A young man heard what I had to say, prayed about it and asked God to give him a creative idea. The pastor called me a few days ago and informed me that the young man had invented a security device that the United States Government is purchasing the rights to use. That witty invention made him an instant multi-millionaire.

What is it that frustrates you? What gets your attention? What causes you pain?

That's how you recognize an opportunity.

_____ 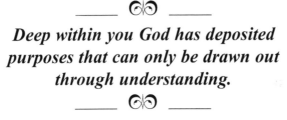 _____

Deep within you God has deposited purposes that can only be drawn out through understanding.

_____ 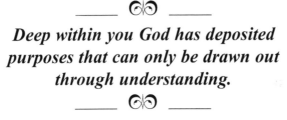 _____

Have you ever walked into Wal-Mart, looked at a product on the shelf and said, "Wait a minute—*that was my idea!*"?

Someone had the same frustration, the same pain, the same problem that you had—but instead of complaining about it, they invented a solution for it. And because they drew the idea out and manufactured it, they received man's currency for their efforts.

When you learn to operate in God's currency of creativity and receive ideas for witty inventions, you will find that wealth is within you awaiting your discovery.

George Washington Carver, the son of a Missouri slave, lifted a handful of peanuts praying, "Great God of the

Universe, Creator of the heavens and the earth, reveal to me the secrets that you housed in the peanut." Then he created over 300 usable and marketable products from that plant.

After that, Carver turned his attention to the sweet potato, again petitioning God for creativity. This one man literally resurrected the economy of the South because of his ability to receive God's currency of creativity.

Do you realize that the future economy lies in what is now hidden in mankind?

The fortunes which will be created by receiving God's currency will be enormous.

The billionaires of the next decade are ordinary people today—just like you and me—but soon they will uncover their hidden creativity, discover a new idea or design a witty invention that will change the world of tomorrow.

God's creative power is yours for the asking.

14 GOD'S CURRENCY: LEADERSHIP

*And Deborah, a prophetess, the wife of Lapidoth,
she judged Israel at that time. And she dwelt
under the palm tree of Deborah between Ramah
and Bethel in mount Ephraim: and the children
of Israel came up to her for judgment.*
Judges 4:4-5

For twenty years King Jabin oppressed the people of Israel.
Their misery reached a pinnacle that caused them to cry out
to the Lord for help. Any time people are oppressed, God
will raise up a leader to move them out of their suffering.
This time God chose a prophetess named Deborah.

Deborah was a great leader; she was instructed in God's
currency of leadership. Deborah judged the people of
Israel. She helped them resolve their differences, decide
their disputes and correct their abuses.

Once her leadership was well established, she ordered
Barak to take an army and overcome Israel's oppressor.
Barak's reply was interesting.

*And Barak said unto her, If thou wilt go with me,
then I will go: but if thou wilt not go with me,
then I will not go.*
Judges 4:8

Barak understood the principles of leadership, but he needed Deborah's ability to move the people to act courageously. Deborah replied to him that she would go with the army, but she chided Barak for his failure to step into a leadership role and declared that the honor Barak could have gained in the battle would be given to a woman instead. God's people prevailed, and Deborah and Jael, the wife of Heber, were credited with the victory.

Any gathering of men requires leadership, and leaders should have their rewards.

Of recent years there has been a lot of criticism directed toward excessive compensation paid to the CEOs of large corporations. I agree that sometimes the dollar amounts can seem outrageous; however, I also know that shareholders have a choice in the matter. They don't have to invest their money into companies with such liberal policies. But what I do appreciate is when a man or woman takes the helm of a company that is facing bankruptcy and is able to turn it around and make enormous profits. A leader deserves the reward of the risk he takes.

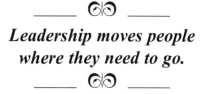

Leadership moves people where they need to go.

Leadership moves people not where they *want* to go, but where they *need* to go.

David was anointed to be the King of Israel at a young age. At the anointing service conducted by the prophet Samuel, the Spirit of the Lord came upon David in power (I Samuel 16:13). Yet the first act of service that David was called to perform was not to lead men, but to play the harp and sing songs.

*If ye have not been faithful in that which is
another man's, who shall give you that which is
your own?*

                                        Luke 16:12

This was a key characteristic of David's leadership. David
proved himself to be faithful in Saul's business. He did not
dishonor Saul's position of leadership.

*David went out whithersoever Saul sent him, and
behaved himself wisely: and Saul set him over the
men of war, and he was accepted in the sight of all
the people, and also in the sight of Saul's servants.*

                                        1 Samuel 18:5

The amicable relationship of Saul and David deteriorated
following David's victories. Saul became jealous and
violent toward David. Saul was so paranoid that David had
to flee into seclusion.

_____ ๑๑ _____

Leadership that only has followers is a cult.

_____ ๑๑ _____

I've seen great leaders, men of great exploits, battle with
the paranoia of potential. Rather than draw greatness out of
their servants, they oppress, control, dictate and manipulate
them.

**Understand this: Leadership that only has followers is a
cult.**

Agreement and submission should be based upon sound
doctrine and godly character. It is never to be based upon
personality, charisma or involuntary control.

**True leadership ability is proven when it draws
greatness out of ordinary men.**

The men gathering around David were not the well-trained, elite forces of Israel's army but those who were in debt, distressed and discontented with life (I Samuel 22:2). The same men who once were the outcasts of society became hailed as "the mighty men of David."

> *Then Jesus went with them. And when he was now not far from the house, the centurion sent friends to him, saying unto him, Lord, trouble not thyself: for I am not worthy that thou shouldest enter under my roof: Wherefore neither thought I myself worthy to come unto thee: but say in a word, and my servant shall be healed. For I also am a man set under authority, having under me soldiers, and I say unto one, Go, and he goeth; and to another, Come, and he cometh; and to my servant, Do this, and he doeth it. When Jesus heard these things, he marvelled at him, and turned him about, and said unto the people that followed him, I say unto you, I have not found so great faith, no, not in Israel.*
>
> *Luke 7:6-9*

Authority flows *through* leadership, not around it.

During my first church plant it was a daily discipline in my prayer time to pray these words: "Oh, God, give me wisdom and insight about the church that I pastor."

God answered my cry, and I would leave prayer with new understanding concerning my responsibilities. I would make decisions on everything from the finances, to the facilities, to the various outreaches such as the youth and children's ministries. God even gave me insight for the music ministry and the woman's ministry *(neither of which I knew anything about)*.

Then the Lord changed my direction and I became the executive pastor at one of America's largest churches. It was still my discipline to pray daily: "Lord, give me wisdom and insight about the church that I serve."

But I heard nothing.

I made the same request for days, weeks and even a few months. Yet God continued to be silent to me about the church's affairs.

One day, out of frustration, I asked five specific questions regarding problem areas that I knew the church was facing. I wrote the requests in my prayer journal and prayed: "Oh, God, give me wisdom and insight about the church. Here are five questions that I have."

Still I heard nothing.

I was perplexed. I said to myself, "I might have missed God by coming here."

Later that day I asked my pastor to go to lunch with me. We went to our favorite Mexican restaurant. While eating chips and salsa, my pastor began to speak. As he talked, he answered the first question that I had prayed about in secret.

Then he answered the second question. The third answer soon followed. During our time together at lunch, my pastor answered all five of the questions I had put before the Lord.

Then I realized, "I'm a man under authority. God is not going to speak *around* leadership. He is going to speak *through* leadership!" I remembered the story about the centurion who approached Jesus with a request for his servant.

In the Bible, centurions have played an important role in Christianity. It was a centurion at the crucifixion of Christ who proclaimed, ***"Truly this was the Son of God"*** (Luke 27:34).

The first Gentile convert recorded in scripture was a centurion (Acts 10:1, 22).

The Roman centurion was a well-conditioned man able to carry approximately 90 pounds of equipment more than twenty miles in a day under the harshest conditions. He wasn't a novice. He was a professional soldier.

Being men of the military, centurions understood leadership. *(In our day, it is said that West Point Military Academy has produced more CEOs than Harvard, Yale and Princeton combined.)*

The centurion in Luke chapter seven understood how to draw upon God's currency of leadership. He approached Jesus with the proper protocol. He requested that Jesus simply give the order, or "just say the word." Rather than expecting Jesus to be present in his home, he simply requested an order of authority to be given.

The centurion's request was not for himself but on behalf of his servant. There is a principle in this story that you need to grasp.

God places you under leadership so you can master what he has put you over.

The Centurion's position of authority was not to rule people and dictate orders, but to allow what was above him to flow to what was beneath him (Matthew 20:25).

Legitimate authority brings benefits in the lives of servants:

*   The benefit of power. Although the Centurion was a man of authority he lacked power to heal his servant. He had to ask the authority above him to flow that power through him.

*   The benefit of protection. Legitimate authority looks for ways to shelter and protect those who serve it (Psalm 91:1).

- The benefit of provision. *"Who serves as a soldier at his own expense?" I Corinthians 9:7*

- The benefit of promotion. The natural process of following great leaders should result in becoming better by default.

  - *He who walks with the wise grows wise. Proverbs 13:20*

  - *Everyone who is fully trained will be like his teacher. Luke 6:40*

God places you under leadership so you can master what He has put you over.

I conduct *"Marketplace Ministry"* meetings throughout the country. These gatherings of entrepreneurs and professionals are some of the most fulfilling meetings that I have ever had, because, in them, I get to influence influencers.

As I teach this message I call, "The Centurion Leadership Principle," I see leaders stepping up to their God-given places of authority. They begin to take their positions of servant leadership and realize the purposes of their positions.

I'm not saying that God-ordained leadership doesn't have its challenges.

Let's face it; everyone loves a leader until something goes wrong. That's when we must delve even deeper into God's currency of leadership and show courage.

David charged Solomon, his son and successor, saying, *"Be strong. Show yourself a man!"* (1 Kings 2:2)

Paul told Timothy, his son in the faith, *"Be strong in the grace that is in Christ Jesus. And the things you have heard me say in the presence of many witnesses entrust to reliable men who will also be qualified to teach others. Endure hardship with us like a good soldier in Christ Jesus" (II Timothy 2:1-3 NIV).*

Anointed leadership is a currency of God (I Corinthians 12:28).

Many people do not realize how important this currency is in their lives. Godly leadership will prosper you when you submit to it.

The key word is to **submit. (Note that submission is only required when you *don't* agree with the leader.** When you agree, there's no problem with committing yourself to obey.)

To submit to something is a voluntary attitude of giving in, cooperating, assuming responsibility and carrying a burden.

> *Anyone who receives instruction in the word must share all good things with his instructor.*
> *Galatians 6:6 NIV*

The currency of God flows into your life to bring increase when you submit to godly leadership.

15 GOD'S CURRENCY: ECONOMIC STRATEGIES

> *And Laban said unto him, I pray thee, if I have found favour in thine eyes, tarry: for I have learned by experience that the LORD hath blessed me for thy sake.*
>
> *Genesis 30:27*

We're all familiar with this story. Jacob received the blessing from his father, Isaac, yet he was forced to flee his home, fearing his brother's wrath.

During the time he was away, Jacob served Laban, his father-in-law, without receiving pay raises or partnership. Fearing that he would lose the blessing associated with his son-in-law, Laban offered to raise Jacob's salary in order to convince Jacob to stay. Of course, Jacob recognized that this was an empty promise. Through all years that Jacob had faithfully served Laban, Laban had cheated Jacob out of his wages ten times.

But Jacob agreed to stay on one condition. Jacob wanted a commission. He wanted to receive compensation directly from what he had produced.

Jacob agreed to take all of the speckled goats and dark-colored lambs rather than the choice colored animals.

> *Jacob, however, took fresh-cut branches from poplar, almond and plane trees and made white stripes on them by peeling the bark and exposing the white inner wood of the branches. Then he placed the peeled branches in all the watering troughs, so that they would be directly in front of the flocks when they came to drink. When the flocks were in heat and came to drink, they mated in front of the branches. And they bore young that were streaked or speckled or spotted.*
> *Genesis 30:37-39 NIV*

Jacob's economic strategy was probably not something that business schools would teach. This is the kind of strategy that requires God's intervention. I can't explain how it worked, but it did. I don't know the process of the miracle. I don't know if the tree branches even had anything to do with what happened, other than that Jacob had faith that they would work. I just know that God gave Jacob a particular economic strategy that prospered him.

God's currency provides economic strategies and financial plans for you.

I will say that when you are looking to prosper, you should consider taking *commission-based earnings,* if possible. You should take the limits off of your work. Great efforts should produce great returns.

God's currency provides economic strategies and financial plans for you.

After leaving office, President George H. W. Bush was the invited guest speaker of a new Japanese corporation. The company offered President Bush a few thousand shares of their company stock in the place of his typical speaker's fee of $200,000. President Bush agreed to receive the stock, and it turned into millions of dollars of income for him.

Now, I'm not saying you should go out and buy all the shares of stock from upstart Japanese companies you can get a hold of. What I am saying is that the work you do should provide more than enough for you to accomplish your divine purpose in life.

> *He who works his land will have abundant food,*
> *but he who chases fantasies lacks judgment.*
> *Proverbs 12:11 NIV*

Commission-based increase is a key to abundance. Just as a seed produces a thirty-, sixty- or even a hundred-fold harvest, commission-based earnings can take the limits off of your income and multiply it exponentially.

In between the cities of Tampa and Orlando in Florida, lives an eccentric multi-millionaire named Kermit Weeks. He owns a few thousand acres of land he named "Orlampa." What is notable about Mr. Weeks is the way he accumulated his fortune.

Years ago, Weeks' grandfather invented a device to increase the production capacity on oil wells. An oil company offered to purchase the rights to the device, but rather than receiving a lump-sum payment from the company, Weeks' grandfather asked for a royalty on the use of the device. During his lifetime Weeks' grandfather only received a few thousand dollars benefit from this decision, however, over time, his invention became so widely used that Kermit Weeks and this man's other grandchildren now receive hundreds of thousands of dollars in royalty payments each month.

When God called me into the ministry I was working in a coalmine in Oklahoma. For a lack of education and experience, I had a good job making a decent hourly wage. To make more money simply meant that I had to work longer hours. Being single, I choose to work an average of 84 hours a week. But then my life changed. God called me into the ministry.

In the fall of 1983, I arrived in Springfield, Missouri, to attend Bible College. I immediately looked in the classified ads section of the newspaper for a job to provide for my basic needs. I landed the job at the car wash I mentioned at the beginning of this book.

At first, I didn't expect much out of the job. The first few days I vacuumed out the cars and I was paid minimum wage. After a week or so, I was promoted to drying cars off. Then I received an hourly wage plus tips. Shortly after that, I was promoted to a position in sales. At the time I didn't realize how significant this promotion would be. I had never sold anything in my life, and I certainly didn't know how to sell a car wash.

My manager encouraged me, saying, "Neil, people want a basic wash, but if you sell them a wax for one dollar more, we'll pay you 50% commission for that wax."

I struggled along for a few days, when I asked Kay (we were dating at the time) to agree with me for God to favor me in my sales. That prayer revolutionized my job!

The first person who came in to the wash looked at the menu and asked for the "Works." I had never sold a "Works" before. It cost $19.95! I was amazed.

Then a second person came in and asked for a wash. I humbly suggested the "Works." Sure enough, he bought it.

A third person came in. I boldly recommended the "Works."

Within an hour, after selling nineteen "Works" packages, my manager ran out of the office and asked me what I was doing.

I was honest and I said that I didn't know.

He said that whatever it was that I was doing, I should just keep doing it.

The next day, I met with Kay and asked her to pray with me again.

Within months I became the sales manager at that car wash and made more money than I had ever dreamed possible. The company had to adjust my salary seven different times to lower my compensation.

Hebrews 11:6 tells us that we must believe that God is a rewarder of those who diligently seek Him. If we believe God is a rewarder and that He truly wants to bless us, whenever we have the opportunity, we should choose commission-based wages. **God's economic strategies will lead us to the best ways for us to prosper.**

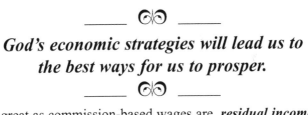

God's economic strategies will lead us to the best ways for us to prosper.

As great as commission-based wages are, *residual income* is even better.

Residual income is simply the best way to earn money for the rest of your life. Jerry Seinfeld will be making money off of the syndication of his television show for decades to come. In like manner, every time a song is played on the radio, a singer goes to the bank.

When you receive residual income, you are paid repeatedly for effort exercised once.

I played golf at Pebble Beach for a charity event with famed producer Michael Omartian. I confess how foolish I felt when I inquired about his career. I don't know much about music, and my ignorance gave me away in my conversation. Michael humbly told me about some of the songs that he had produced. Amazingly they were all songs that I grew up hearing. Each time one of the hundreds of songs that he has written or produced is played on the radio, a check is mailed to his home! That's residual income.

I have consulted for several entrepreneurs down through the years. I have encouraged each one of them to look carefully into developing a plan for receiving residual income.

One particular friend of my ministry is one of the brightest and most skilled persons that I know. For years he worked diligently to make a living. One day I encouraged him and said, "You need to discover a service in your industry so you can be paid regularly for what you do one time." Together we prayed for wisdom. Not long after that, he called me with a great idea—what I would call a "God-idea." Without exaggeration, he's on a pace to make millions of dollars in just a few years off the residual income that this idea will produce.

Now, let's go back to the story of Jacob. Not only did Jacob see that commission-based income would provide a great avenue of blessing for him, he also understood the importance of establishing a source of residual income.

> *Art thou greater than our father Jacob, which gave us the well, and drank thereof himself, and his children, and his cattle?*
>
> *John 4:12*

Even is Jesus' day, the Samaritan woman at the well was continuing to be supplied with water from a well that Jacob had dug hundreds of years earlier.

Someone else laid the foundations before us and we continue to be blessed by them.

Another variation of God's currency in economic strategy is similar to residual income, but it is even better—it's *passive income.*

To receive passive income means that you get paid for some activity, but you did not actively participate in the generation of that income. When you invest in stocks or bonds, for example, you don't use the sweat of your brow to generate income, but you are using money to make money. Your money is generating income for you.

A young couple approached me during a service one day and handed me a sizable envelope with several hundred dollars in it. They said they were sowing seed for a new idea (God's currency) for a business.

_____ ☉ _____

It's a great day in your life when you become an investor and not just a consumer.

_____ ☉ _____

The man shared with me that he had recently lost the patent for a product that he invented to a large corporation. Rather than sue the corporation, he decided that he would learn from his mistake and replace his invention with a new idea. The next day, he went to the shore of the Bay of Mobile, sat down and began to pray. Within a few hours, he received not only an idea for a product, but a strategy to make it and license it to others. He followed through on the plan God gave him and soon became very wealthy.

It's a great day in your life when you become an investor and not just a consumer.

> *For the LORD thy God blesseth thee, as he promised thee: and thou shalt lend unto many nations, but thou shalt not borrow; and thou shalt reign over many nations, but they shall not reign*

over thee.

Deuteronomy 15:6

Another key economic strategy God designed for your
benefit is the use of *multiple streams of income.*

*The LORD hath blessed my master greatly; and he
is become great: and he hath given him flocks,
and herds, and silver, and gold, and menservants,
and maidservants, and camels, and asses.*

Genesis 24:35

As I mentioned in an earlier chapter, Abraham knew the
secret of God's blessing through multiple streams of
income. Not only did he have sheep, he had cattle. He had
gold and he had silver. He had menservants and
maidservants. He had the two existing forms of
transportation—camels and asses. He used each stream of
income to bring blessing into his life.

If gold hit a low point in the marketplace, Abraham had
silver to fall back on. If there was a shortage of water, he
had camels to trade and sell to traveling merchants rather
than donkeys. This made Abraham's overall income
extremely stable. If one channel of revenue dried up or
suffered an economic hardship, another stream would take
up the slack. Abraham held a diversified portfolio with
eight different streams of income.

*Divide what you have into seven parts, or even
into eight, because you don't know what disaster
may happen on earth.*

Ecclesiastes 11:2 GOD'S WORD

When God opens the storehouse of His bounty. He pours
out multiple streams of blessing on His obedient children
(Malachi 3:10).

Developing a personal storehouse is another one of God's
economic strategies for blessing His people.

...He who gathers money little by little makes it grow.

Proverbs 13:11 NIV

God wants to bless your storehouse, but you must have one before He can do so.

Saving money is a discipline that rewards itself. **It requires an act of faith for a person to deny current needs to save for future wants.**

That is exactly what immigrants do when they come to America. They come with an attitude that they must save pennies now in order to enjoy dollars later. Those of us who are multi-generational Americans have the disadvantage of privilege. Prosperity actually has worked against us.

The laborer's appetite works for him; his hunger drives him on.

Proverbs 16:26 NIV

The late Pastor John Osteen taught God's people the principle of "living off the top of the barrel." This principle simply means that you should work toward living on the overflow of your capital.

In other words never consume your base, but live on the interest your money produces. Any future income enlarges your capital base and therefore gives you a raise in your standard of living.

I believe this is a brilliant plan. It takes patience to create the framework in your life; however, once it is in place and adhered to diligently, you, your family and your descendents after you will always be prosperous.

THE APPLICATION

❧❧

A DEVOTIONAL
GUIDE TO GOD'S BLESSINGS

16 A DEVOTIONAL GUIDE TO GOD'S BLESSING

AN INTRODUCTION

As I mentioned before, the Queen of Sheba traveled hundreds of miles from her home under difficult circumstances to the land of Israel in order to seek the wisdom Solomon had to offer. She came to him with numerous questions and an enormous caravan of gifts as a profound demonstration of her hunger for guidance.

Astounded by the wisdom of Solomon, when the queen returned to her native land, it is said that she introduced the worship of the true God of Israel into her culture. It is obvious that her seed prospered, because we find in the Book of Acts that the Ethiopian Secretary of Treasury (a descendant of Sheba) traveled the same ancient path as his ancestral queen in order to worship the God of Israel in Jerusalem. Philip, the evangelist, was divinely sent to him, told him the Good News concerning Jesus, and baptized the diplomat in water.

Unlike the people who lived in Bible times, God's wisdom is available to us in abundance today like never before in history. We not only have the opportunity to read the wisdom Solomon wrote by divine inspiration in the Book of Proverbs, but we have an entire Bible to read any time we chose in any translation and language we want, as well as, a multitude of tools and study guides available to us so we can virtually immerse ourselves in the thoughts and plans of God.

My prayer for you is that the devotional section of this book will be a tool to lead you to understand God's great wisdom and plan for blessing in your life.

Just as there are 31 chapters in the book of Proverbs—one for each day of the month—I have included 31 very brief financial devotions for you to read, study and meditate upon to help you begin to develop a vision of God's plan for your success and prosperity. The simple truths and prayers in these devotions can be a reference for you to return to over and over again in your search for God's plan concerning your finances. I challenge you to read and act on one of these devotions each day for the next month and unlock the blessings God has in store for you.

Be blessed!

— Neil Kennedy —

1 SUSTAINING DECISIONS BY FAITH

By faith Abraham, when God tested him, offered Isaac as a sacrifice. He who had received the promises was about to sacrifice his one and only son, even though God had said to him, "It is through Isaac that your offspring will be reckoned."

Hebrews 11:17-18 NIV

When making decisions in life, it is imperative that we sustain those decisions through faith in the Word of God. The Word of God must be implemented and meditated upon daily. Death and destruction, or even the *appearance* of them, will try to rob us and keep us from receiving God's promises, but faith in God's Word will override negative appearances and lead us to obey.

Because his decision was anchored by faith in God's Word, Abraham was able to sustain the life of his son. Abraham had received God's promise and therefore reasoned that God was able and willing to raise Isaac from the dead if he obeyed God's request. Abraham knew God was more powerful than death, so he made the decision to obey God's Word by faith.

Faith in God's Word is needed to sustain any decision we make. Making wise financial decisions requires faith in God's promise to bless us despite the *appearance* that we may be giving something up in the short term. The decisions to tithe faithfully and give offerings out of obedience must be based upon the foundation of what God says in His Word. Remember this principle: Anything that dies in Christ—a promise, a God-given desire, or even a tithe—will be resurrected and glorified.

Father, I thank You for the wisdom you have given me today. I declare that I not only have

faith to make the right decisions in the area of
tithes and offerings, but I am able to sustain those
decisions by faith. I am able to see what may be
called "dead" to me become resurrected and
glorified through your power. I am making the
decision today to live by faith in Your Word, in
Jesus' Name. Amen. ☙☙

2 BLESSED BY THE GREATER

And without all contradiction the less is blessed of
the better. And here men that die receive tithes;
but there he receiveth them, of whom it is
witnessed that he liveth.

Hebrews 7:7-8

One common misunderstanding regarding the tithe is that
we are in the superior position of blessing the church with
it. In reality, it is *God* who blesses *us* with the opportunity
to tithe.

Hebrews 7:7-8 teaches that the "lesser is blessed by the
greater." We know that God is far greater than any man. In
addition, these verses teach us that Jesus is the one who
receives our tithes. God's plan for us to put ourselves in
position to receive His blessings is for us to put our tithes
into the hands of His Son.

When we withhold our tithes, we are actually robbing God.
He says in Malachi 3:10 that one purpose of the tithe is to
meet the needs of the house of God. I Timothy 3:15 refers
to the church as the "house of God." Accordingly, we must
pay our tithe to the church, giving cheerfully at the
opportunity to worship our Lord. In return, God will open
up the windows of Heaven to us and pour out a blessing
that we cannot contain.

Lord, I believe that You are literally receiving my
tithe, according to Hebrews 7:8. I worship You
with everything that I am, everything that I have,
and everything that I do. My tithe represents my
life. It represents who I am and what I've done. I
magnify You with it, and receive your blessings
now, in Jesus' Name. Amen. ◔◔

3 THE BASICS OF TITHING

And he blessed him, and said, Blessed be Abram
of the most high God, possessor of heaven and
earth: And blessed be the most high God, which
hath delivered thine enemies into thy hand. And
he gave him tithes of all.
Genesis 14:19-20

There are several basic principles of tithing we can glean
from this scripture. The first is that **the tithe is a tenth of
our income.**

Once in a church I pastored, we had a new convert coming
to every service, three times each week. Mistakenly, yet
joyfully, he was giving ten percent of his income in the
offering in every service! He misunderstood the Biblical
command to give ten percent and thought that giving this
amount was a requirement for attending our church.
Although this man will be blessed for his liberality, he was
probably relieved when he discovered that giving that
amount in each service was not a required by God.

Another area of confusion for some is in deciding whether
they should pay their tithe **before or after** they have paid
their taxes.

The answer is simple. If we want our taxes to be blessed,
we should tithe on the full amount, always putting God
first.

We also learn that **the tithe is holy**. It must be paid completely and consistently. Tithing enables us to go to God in prayer and produce our testimony against the devourer.

Lastly, we see that **the tithe is a matter of faith.** Many people believe the tithe is just Old Testament Law, but in Genesis 14, Abraham tithed before the Law was ever given. We operate by the faith of Abraham and tithe because we are blessed of God.

> ***Father, I confess that I am blessed. I have a great future, Lord, because I am controlling my financial destiny with the tithe. I thank You, Father, that even in the midst of those who would propagate fear and uncertainty, I am not fearful or uncertain. I simply commit myself to obedience in faith, and I thank You that I am blessed, in Jesus' Name. Amen.***

4 God Is Our Source

> ***The king of Sodom said to Abram, "Give me the people and keep the goods for yourself." But Abram said to the king of Sodom, "I have raised my hand to the LORD, God Most High, Creator of heaven and earth, and have taken an oath that I will accept nothing belonging to you, not even a thread or the thong of a sandal, so that you will never be able to say, 'I made Abram rich.'"***
>
> ***Genesis 14:21-23 NIV***

God is the only source of true prosperity and He is far more capable of blessing us than any man.

God had blessed Abram, and as a result, Abram gave back to God. Abram did not align himself with the wicked. He was unwilling to share the glory of his prosperity by affiliating himself with the king of Sodom. The king of Sodom ruled a wicked city, on which judgment would later fall.

Abram knew God was his source and that wealth from wicked men was not needed for him to prosper. By refusing the king of Sodom's offer, Abram made sure that God, and God alone, would receive the glory for his prosperity. God is the source of true promotion and blessing.

> *Wealth gotten by vanity shall be diminished: but he that gathereth by labour shall increase.*
> *Proverbs 13:11*

Like faithful Abram, we must also seek God as the source of our prosperity and refuse business alliances which compromise our faith. The Bible tells us that ill-gotten gain is not lasting.

> *Father, I thank You that You are the true source of my promotion and prosperity. I will not compromise or bow to the pressures of ungodly men. I seek to do Your will and to glorify You in all that I do. I don't seek after money for money's sake, but I obey Your Word and give my tithes and offerings back to You in return for the blessings You have poured out on my life, in Jesus' Name. Amen.*

5 THE TITHE IS HOLY

> *A tithe of everything from the land, whether grain from the soil or fruit from the trees, belongs to the LORD; it is holy to the LORD. If a man redeems any of his tithe, he must add a fifth of the value to it.*
> *Leviticus 27:30-31 NIV*

The tithe is holy and it is sanctified for a purpose. The purpose of tithing the firstfruits of our increase is to show priority to God and to His work.

As a result of our putting God first in our finances, God will bring increase back to us again. He will not only bless the 10% of our finances we've given, but He will also bless the remaining 90%. We can do far more with 90% of a blessed income than we could ever do with 100% of a cursed income. When we tithe to God, He blesses us with the sanctified use of our finances, and we are destined for increase.

There is a penalty for ignoring the purpose of the tithe. Based on Leviticus 27:30, if we "redeem" any of our tithe—that means if we take some back or withhold part of it for any reason—we should add an additional 20% to the total we pay to the Lord.

A good illustration of this principle can been seen in the story of Adam and Eve. Adam had his choice of the fruit of all the trees in the Garden of Eden except one. This tree had been sanctified for another purpose—yet Adam ate of it anyway. Adam's sin brought a curse upon all of his descendants.

We have often judged Adam for this sin—but how often do we ignore the sanctified purpose of the tithe?

Our sin concerning the tithe will bring a curse upon our future finances—but our obedience will bring manifold blessings and open God's storehouse of bounty.

> *Father, I thank You that I have increase and my income is blessed. I return unto You the first portion of my increase—the tithe. I honor You because through this exercise of faith, obedience and worship, I am showing my victory over materialism. I give You priority in everything*

concerning my life and my finances, in Jesus'
Name. Amen. ☉◌

6 THE THREE TESTIMONIES OF THE TITHE

The earth is the LORD'S, and the fulness thereof;
the world, and they that dwell therein.
                                        Psalms 24:1

For whatsoever is born of God overcometh the
world: and this is the victory that overcometh the
world, even our faith.
                                        I John 5:4

And I will rebuke the devourer for your sakes, and
he shall not destroy the fruits of your ground;
neither shall your vine cast her fruit before the
time in the field, saith the LORD of hosts.
                                        Malachi 3:11

There are three testimonies we give when we pay the tithe.

First, **the tithe is a testimony to God.** The act of tithing
recognizes that we tithe because we are blessed. We are
testifying that all we have is *because* of God, and all we
have *belongs* to God.

Second **the tithe is a testimony to ourselves.** Paying the
tithe gives testimony to the fact that we have victory over
the lust for wealth in this world. Giving God the firstfruits
of our increase assures us that we are not serving money,
but money is serving us. We have victory over materialism
and greed.

Lastly, **tithing testifies to the devil that he has no
unsettled claims over our money.** Tithing stops the hand
of the devourer from touching our finances.

Father, I thank You that I not only hear Your
Word, but I do Your Word. I testify that all that I
have is because of You. You own everything on
this earth and I am just a steward of Your
blessings. I thank You that materialism and greed
have no place in my life. Money serves me. I am
the master of my finances. I also thank You that
the devourer is stopped in trying to work against
my finances. I testify that blessing and prosperity
follow me as I obey Your Word, in Jesus' Name.
Amen. ෨෩

7 FAILURE IN FINANCES

Jesus continued: "There was a man who had two
sons. The younger one said to his father, 'Father,
give me my share of the estate.' So he divided his
property between them. Not long after that, the
younger son got together all he had, set off for a
distant country and there squandered his wealth
in wild living. After he had spent everything,
there was a severe famine in that whole country,
and he began to be in need. So he went and hired
himself out to a citizen of that country, who sent
him to his fields to feed pigs. He longed to fill his
stomach with the pods that the pigs were eating,
but no one gave him anything."
                                    Luke 15:11-16 NIV

This parable illustrates several things regarding financial
failure. Jesus said the young man gathered *"all he had"*
and left. He saw his inheritance—something his father had
worked long and hard for—as "his share," rather than as a
blessing. His ingratitude was also directed toward God. By
gathering all he had, the scriptures imply that he did not

tithe. He neither honored his earthly father nor his Heavenly Father with thanksgiving.

The scriptures also point out that he *"squandered his wealth."* The young man did not show right relationships to other people or to God in giving. Consequently, during the famine, he had great need.

Proverbs 16:26 says, *"The laborer's appetite works for him; his hunger drives him on"* (NIV). This foolish young man was hungry. He even longed for that which was unclean. But because he was not a giver, no one gave him anything. The young man had broken the principle of Luke 6:38— give and it will be given back to you—and he suffered because of it. Fortunately, the young man had a father who loved him, who forgave him and who restored him to his place in the estate.

Thank God that He, too, will forgive any shortcomings in the area of tithing. If we've been disobedient and selfish, God will allow us to return to a right financial relationship with Him, and His blessings will abound.

> *Thank You, Father, for Your grace. Thank You for all the times You have given to me, even though I have shown ingratitude. Thank You that if I've disobeyed Your Word, I can return to You today and see Your hand of forgiveness and blessing upon me. Thank You for restoring me to a place of honor and right standing, in Jesus' Name. Amen.*

8 The Law Of Progressive Increase

> *Dear friend, I pray that you may enjoy good health and that all may go well with you, even as your soul is getting along well.*
>
> **III John 2 NIV**

Beloved, I wish above all things that thou mayest prosper and be in health, even as thy soul prospereth.

III John 2 KJV

The Word of God teaches a law of progressive increase. It states that as we put the Word of God into our lives, mixing it with faith, we will make progress and have increase.

In other words, the revelation and increase we have, comes from the Word of God. If we want more revelation and increase, we must work on our spirit man. By training our minds, wills and emotions with the Word of God, we strengthen our souls. Health and prosperity are by-products of inward strength. Focusing on growing spiritually guarantees health and increase in our lives.

In Job 1:9, satan asked, "Does Job fear God for nothing?"

He was accusing Job of worshiping God only for the sake of money. When we tithe and give offerings cheerfully, satan can not make such accusations. He no longer has a claim on our finances.

As we increase in the spiritual realm, by reading and meditating on God's Word and by obeying the principles of tithing and giving, increase in the natural realm will come our way. Our blessings are not a result of our own merit but of God's goodness and grace. Whatever level we're at—whether our tithe is $10 or $10,000—we must remain faithful. We will be blessed spiritually and financially.

Lord, I thank You for the opportunity to worship You. I thank you that as I grow in Your Word, You continue to bless me. I thank You that health and prosperity are mine, even as my soul prospers. I commit to increase my spiritual strength and to focus on my relationship with You. Give me revelation, wisdom and spiritual might, so that I may be a doer of Your Word. I have confidence that You are blessing me and everything I put my hands to, in Jesus' Name. Amen. ☉☉

9 Reaping A Bountiful Harvest

Remember this: Whoever sows sparingly will also reap sparingly, and whoever sows generously will also reap generously.
II Corinthians 9:6 NIV

Did you ever stop to think about the fact that the difference between a garden and a field is simply how many seeds are planted in it?

If you just plant a garden, you're a gardener. You can't call yourself a farmer.

The way we plant is the way we'll receive. If we want to reap a really big harvest, we must sow large amounts of seed. This principle isn't just for vegetables. It's also true in the area of finances.

Another principle that determines the size of a farmer's harvest is his carefulness to plant his seed in the proper way at the proper time in the proper location for the particular crop he wants to grow. A huge crop of watermelons cannot be reaped from the Mojave Desert in the middle of August.

The spiritual correlation to this is that if God tells us to give something a certain way or to a certain place, He won't let us get by with disobeying or trying to skirt the issue. No harvest of blessing can come from disobedience. What God said in His Word, and how we act upon it, determines whether or not we will receive the financial harvest He has promised. Jesus literally *is* the Word of God, and He will not turn away from what He has said,even if it's just in order to bless us. The Word is clear that the primary avenue of blessing God uses to bring harvest into our lives is the tithe, and the place it is to be planted is the church.

Just as a PIN number allows you to withdraw money from your bank account here on earth, the tithe is like your personal identification number into the accounts of Heaven. We cannot bypass this area in our lives and expect to receive God's abundant harvest in our finances.

> *Lord, I thank You that You are true to Your Word. You said if I would sow bountifully, I would reap a bountiful harvest. I commit myself to honor You with the firstfruits of my income and with the offerings You direct me to give in the places and times You direct me to give them. I believe You will bless everything I set my hands to because of my obedience. I honor You in the area of sowing financial seed, in Jesus' Name. Amen.* ☉☉

10 Giving From The Heart

> *Each man should give what he has decided in his heart to give, not reluctantly or under compulsion, for God loves a cheerful giver.*
> **II Corinthians 9:7 NIV**

It is with his heart that a man makes the quality decision to give. While men may look on the outward appearance of things, the Bible says that God always looks on the heart. When we make the decision to become generous and cheerful givers from our hearts, God is ecstatic!

In His earthly walk, Jesus took notice of people's giving. When the poor, widow woman gave 1/40 of a penny, Jesus called this to the attention of all of His disciples. Although many before her gave much greater amounts, she was the one He commended. Though her gift was small, it was all that she had. Jesus accounted it to her as if she had given more than any of the rich people surrounding her. He discerned that her gift truly came from her heart.

In the news today, we hear many stories of how celebrities and top executives have donated large amounts of money to different social causes. Recently one man even announced that he was making a gift of more than three million dollars to a particular relief organization. While that's certainly a lot of money, this man's net worth is somewhere around sixty billion dollars. His gift wasn't even close to the tithe. In God's eyes, the poor widow still has this man beat in the area of giving from the heart.

Jesus gave Himself to the world because He loved us. We must also give from a heart of love. We must not give "reluctantly or under compulsion." We should neither *hesitate* to give, or be *driven* to give. When we make the decision to give from the heart, we will become cheerful givers, and God will be overjoyed.

> *Lord, I thank You that I can make the choice to tithe and to give out of a heart of love for You. My gifts to Your kingdom purposes are true acts of worship. Because I am created in Your image and You are a great giver, I thank You that I can be a great giver, too. I confess that I am a cheerful giver, therefore, You love me and You pour out Your favor and blessings in my life, in Jesus' Name. Amen.* ☺☺

11 Grace In Giving

> *And God is able to make all grace abound toward you; that ye, always having all sufficiency in all things, may abound to every good work.*
> *II Corinthians 9:8*

God promises to give us grace in the area of giving. To receive God's grace is to have His divine favor placed upon our lives.

When we become givers, God is able to bless us with His divine favor and power. His grace will bring us favor in our purchases, in our transactions and in our dealings with others. But take note that II Corinthians 9:8 promises this abounding grace only to those who are willing to give their resources to invest in the lives of others. God's abundant favor and power work on the behalf of the man who is a giver.

> *"Give, and it will be given to you. A good measure, pressed down, shaken together and running over, will be poured into your lap. For with the measure you use, it will be measured to you."*
>
> *Luke 6:38 NIV*

Giving brings a never-ending supply of God's grace. When we bless others, God, in turn, sends someone to bless us, so that we may bless others again. God's grace will overflow in the life of a giver to the point that he will *always* have *all* sufficiency in *all* things, so that he may continue to give to *every* good work.

I don't know about you, but I want that kind of grace in my life!

> *Lord, thank You for the opportunity to receive Your grace in the area of giving. Thank You that You have given me divine favor. Thank You for blessing me to overflowing so that I might continue to be a blessing and come to the point where I can give to every good work. I look for, and expect, even more blessing in the days ahead, in Jesus' Name. Amen.*

12 FINANCING A VISION

The Israelites did as Moses instructed and asked the Egyptians for articles of silver and gold and for clothing. The LORD had made the Egyptians favorably disposed toward the people, and they gave them what they asked for; so they plundered the Egyptians.

Exodus 12:35-36 NIV

According to the Word, the wealth of the unrighteous is laid up just to be handed over to the righteous. The Israelites who left Egypt received 400 years of back pay for their labor in one day!

God gave the Israelites a vision to begin new lives in a land He had promised them. He delivered them out of captivity and supernaturally provided the resources they would need to establish His plan by turning the hearts of the Egyptians to favor His people. Like the Israelites, God has given us a great vision—to further His kingdom here on earth. It will take faith in this vision for us to attract visionaries to help us finance it.

God wants to provide for us, but we must believe that the vision He has given us is worthy of an investment. We must believe that the vision will attract the attention of people who will be favorably disposed to sow into it, and we must believe that the vision will lead us to the promises of God.

No vision is more worthy of investment than the preaching of the Gospel of the Lord Jesus Christ, for it is the power of God for men to be saved. The Gospel is the greatest force on earth, and we need to be bold enough to tell the world our cause is a worthy one and to ask for their support.

Lord, please give me boldness and strong faith in the vision You have given me. I believe I have received a purpose from You for my finances that is greater than the bottom line on a spreadsheet. I believe I receive ideas for new business ventures, ideas for how I can become a better employee, and ideas for how I can be blessed and favored by You. Thank You, Father, that the wealth of the unrighteous is being laid up and stored for me so that I can spread the Good News of Jesus Christ, in Jesus' Name. Amen. ◠◠

13 RENEWING OUR MINDS

For my thoughts are not your thoughts, neither are your ways my ways, saith the LORD. For as the heavens are higher than the earth, so are my ways higher than your ways, and my thoughts than your thoughts.

Isaiah 55:8-9

As with other areas in our lives, we need to renew our minds with the Word of God in the area of our finances. We need to train our minds to think the way God thinks, because His ways are much higher and better than ours.

We travel on highways because they are faster, straighter and safer than regular roads. On city streets we encounter stoplights, on-coming traffic and many other distractions that can upset the flow of our driving and delay us from arriving at our destinations. Like highways, God's ways are more efficient in getting us to where we need to go. God's ways allow us to soar past the distractions of life.

The Word of God teaches us that God's way is a higher way of living. It's life on a much higher level than the world's system. In the area of finances, God's way will make us more prosperous. Tithing and sowing financial seed into God's kingdom brings our finances up to a higher place where they are able to be supernaturally blessed. No worldly financial seminar or strategy can offer a better alternative to the increase that is brought into our lives by the tithe. Only God can make us truly prosperous.

> *Thank You, Lord, that You've given me Your thoughts. Thank You that I can learn Your ways from the truth You've revealed to me in Your Word by the Holy Spirit. I commit myself to renew my mind in the area of finances so I can think the way You think and receive the blessings You have in store for me, in Jesus' Name. Amen.* ☉☉

14 The Ability To Prosper

> *But thou shalt remember the LORD thy God: for it is he that giveth thee power to get wealth, that he may establish his covenant which he sware unto thy fathers, as it is this day.*
>
> *Deuteronomy 8:18*

God gives us the power to produce wealth in order to establish His covenant. The purpose of God-given prosperity is to enable us to spread the knowledge of His Word throughout the world.

God uses two types of people to spread His Word: *those who go* and *those who send.* Those who go are great achievers in God's kingdom. Multitudes of them are called to take God's message around the globe. God gives them open doors to preach the Gospel to those who would never be able to hear it any other way.

The works of the ones who go, however, are only made possible through the financial support provided by the second group of people God uses: *those who send.* If you are a tither, you are a sender, providing the means necessary for the Word of God to go around the world. Goers and senders both have vital roles to play in establishing God's covenant on the earth.

Deuteronomy 8:18 reminds us that neither the going nor the sending is possible without God, Himself. He gives the goers the call to reach the world and open doors of utterance, and He gives the senders the power and ability to prosper, enabling us all to have a part in His work.

> *Lord, thank You for giving me the ability to get wealth in order to establish Your covenant on the earth. You have given me the opportunity to be blessed and to prosper. I believe I have the power to receive the provision I need to complete the instructions You have given me: to go into all the world and preach the Good News. Thank You for allowing me to play a part in spreading Your Word, in Jesus' Name. Amen.*

15 CREDITED RIGHTEOUSNESS

> *What does the Scripture say? "Abraham believed God, and it was credited to him as righteousness."*
> *Romans 4:3 NIV*

In our society, it is nearly impossible to live without established credit; without it you may be unable to purchase essential items, and your name is worth very little. Developing a good credit record isn't something you should do just so you can acquire more debt. You need credit to accomplish things in life, to make your name valuable and to demonstrate that your word is good. Good credit lets people know that you are a person who pays your bills and has integrity in your finances.

Just as we need credit in the natural realm, we also need credit in the spiritual realm. Spiritual credit enables us to withdraw that which we've not yet earned. It represents worthiness and integrity, enabling us to accomplish things we would not otherwise be able to accomplish.

The good news is that we acquire spiritual credit through faith—by simply believing God. Abraham received an account full of righteousness because he walked in faith. He received God's promise that he would have a son, yet he and Sarah were unable to have children. Abraham had the spiritual promise, but he did not have the physical potential. But because he believed, Abraham planted seeds of obedience and God credited him with righteousness and made the promise possible.

God wants to credit us in the area of finances. He wants to make our names valuable and enable us to accomplish great things, but we must believe His Word and plant seeds for prosperity. God will turn the impossible into a reality in our lives, if we'll simply believe and obey.

Lord, I thank You that Your Word is true. You've given us a way to draw from Your account of righteousness. Thank You that even in the natural realm of finances, You've given us the opportunity to draw wealth from the promises in Your Word. I believe Your promise and I will obey it so that I might receive the reality of prosperity in my life, in Jesus' Name. Amen.

16 OPENING THE FLOODGATES OF HEAVEN

Bring ye all the tithes into the storehouse, that there may be meat in mine house, and prove me now herewith, saith the LORD of hosts, if I will not open you the windows of heaven, and pour you out a blessing, that there shall not be room enough to receive it.

Malachi 3:10

It is important that we understand what the floodgates of Heaven are, so that we will recognize them when they are opened to us. Open floodgates are God's way of blessing us—or God's currency.

God has entrusted each of us with talents and abilities that can be turned into tangible currency. There are three steps we need to take in order to open Heaven's floodgates, using the talents God has given us. *The first step is discovering what our abilities are.* If we do not know what our abilities are, we cannot master them. Every person can make a contribution if they know their talent.

Next, we need to develop our abilities to their fullest. We need to train and educate ourselves. We should become experts in our fields.

Finally, we need to distribute our abilities to others. God has given us gifts to use to bless humanity. If we properly steward those gifts and bless those around us, God will open up the floodgates of Heaven to us. He will give us wisdom, creative ideas, financial strategies, witty inventions and favor—His currency—to pour out blessings upon us that we cannot contain.

> *Father, thank You that the windows of Heaven are open to me. I thank You that You are giving me the wisdom to discern my special abilities and to sharpen my skills so that I might be a blessing. Thank You that You have given me the ability to turn Your wonderful gifts into tangible currency, in Jesus' Name. Amen.*

17 DIVINE FAVOR THROUGH OBEDIENCE

Ye are cursed with a curse: for ye have robbed me, even this whole nation. Bring ye all the tithes into the storehouse, that there may be meat in

> *mine house, and prove me now herewith, saith the*
> *LORD of hosts, if I will not open you the windows*
> *of heaven, and pour you out a blessing, that there*
> *shall not be room enough to receive it.*
> *Malachi 3:9-10*

Our obedience to God and His Word determines our level of blessing. When we practice the discipline of tithing, we will have favor and promotion. God provides supernatural, divine favor that flows into our lives through obedience.

On the contrary, when we walk in disobedience to God's Word, we bring a curse upon ourselves. God leaves it up to us to determine whether we want to have the blessings of Heaven poured out upon our finances or to have a curse on our money. Our choice to obey will bring us prosperity in such abundance that we will not have the room enough to contain it all.

> *...For Esther did the commandment of Mordecai,*
> *like as when she was brought up with him.*
> *Esther 2:20*

This passage gives us a great example of how obedience positions us to receive divine favor. Esther was marked with a favor purposed of God. It brought her immediate promotion, prosperity and protection. She obeyed the instructions that were given to her. It was her obedience that brought her divine favor. Her divine favor put her in such a high position that she was able to deliver an entire race of people from potential holocaust.

> *Lord, thank You that You've given me the*
> *opportunity to chose blessing or cursing for my*
> *finances. I choose blessing. I will obey Your*
> *commandment to bring my tithes into Your*
> *storehouse. Thank You that the opened windows*
> *of Heaven pour out divine favor to go to work in*
> *my life. Thank You that through the tithe, I have*

protection, prosperity and promotion, in Jesus'
Name. Amen. ⟳⟲

18 MINISTERING SPIRITS

> *Are not all angels ministering spirits sent to serve*
> *those who will inherit salvation?*
> > *Hebrews 1:14 NIV*

The Word is clear. God has assigned angels to serve us and
to make our ways prosperous. Specifically, He has sent his
angels to do several things on our behalf.

First, ***they are to go ahead of us and make our journeys***
successful. Abraham's servant went ahead to look for his
son's wife. Abraham knew that an angel was assigned to
make his servant's trip prosperous and the servant returned
with a beautiful young woman to help Isaac propagate the
Jewish race. Exodus 23:20 records that the Lord sent an
angel before His people when they left Egypt to help them
to get to the place He had prepared for them.

Angels are also assigned to deliver provisions. When
Elijah was in need, twice an angel brought food and
prepared it for him (I Kings 19). The supplies the angel
brought him enabled the prophet to supernaturally travel for
forty days from its strength.

Angels are also assigned to our safety. Angels are sent to
watch over God's seed. They stop the mouths of lions,
destroy invading armies and watch over even the smallest
child in God's kingdom.

> ***For he will command his angels concerning you***
> ***to guard you in all your ways.***
> > *Psalm 91:11 NIV*

God has angels at the ready to take care of us in every
area—even in the area of our finances.

*Thank You, Lord, for assigning ministering
spirits—Your angels—to help make my way
successful. I thank You that You have divine
appointments for me to keep and Your angels will
help me to prosper in my way. You said in Your
Word that many have entertained angels unaware,
and I believe that Your ministering spirits are at
work in my life, directing me, providing for me
and protecting me every day, in Jesus' Name.
Amen.* ◉◉

19 GOD'S PROTECTION OF OUR WEALTH

*And I will rebuke the devourer for your sakes, and
he shall not destroy the fruits of your ground;
neither shall your vine cast her fruit before the
time in the field, saith the LORD of hosts.*
Malachi 3:11

In some areas of the country, every homeowner is required
to have an insurance bond protecting their home against
termites. In other areas, the government provides flood
insurance for homeowners to purchase. Every state in
America requires that licensed drivers have certain amounts
of vehicle liability insurance coverage on their automobiles.

An insurance policy provides its owner with financial
protection from unforeseen trouble that might be costly to
repair. Auto insurance pays money to repair a vehicle the
policy owner may have accidentally damaged. Flood
insurance rebuilds a covered structure that was damaged by
a natural disaster involving water. A termite insurance bond
certifies that a house has been treated and is protected from
pests that might get in to the foundation of a home. (You
might not even know you have termites, until one day when
you're walking along and your foot falls through the floor.)

Like an insurance verification card, a certificate of termite
treatment or a printed insurance policy, the tithe
demonstrates the protection of our finances. God says the
tithe will protect our financial foundations—our wealth and
income—from pests. When we tithe, we are not under the
control of disastrous outside circumstances or devouring
pests. When we tithe, God raises us up above negative
natural or supernatural circumstances that would try to rob
us of His provision. Tithing is our guarantee of God's
protection.

> *Thank You, Lord, for protecting me and blessing
> me. Thank You, Father, that I am not under the
> control of negative natural or supernatural
> circumstances and my finances are not subject to
> the pestilence of the enemy. My financial
> foundation is secure because I obey You in the
> tithe, in Jesus' Name. Amen.* ☉☽

20 DWELLING IN A DELIGHTFUL LAND

> *"Bring the whole tithe into the storehouse, that
> there may be food in my house. Test me in this,"
> says the LORD Almighty, "and see if I will not
> throw open the floodgates of heaven and pour out
> so much blessing that you will not have room
> enough for it. I will prevent pests from devouring
> your crops, and the vines in your fields will not
> cast their fruit," says the LORD Almighty. "Then
> all the nations will call you blessed, for yours will
> be a delightful land," says the LORD Almighty.*
> *Malachi 3:10-12 NIV*

God wants our land to be a delightful land, providing
security, surplus, satisfaction and success. When we tithe,
we are secure in our finances. We dwell safely in the
confidence that satan has no unsettled claims over our

finances. The return on our tithe also provides us with surplus. God blesses us with more than enough. When we tithe, God not only blesses our current income, but he brings an increase. In addition, our delightful land is a place of satisfaction and success.

When we tithe, we enter into a place of fulfillment in our finances. Satan fails at any attempt to persuade us that he has something better. We will be deeply satisfied. We don't have to look for the next gimmick or scheme to try to turn a profit. We know that profit comes by planting seed.

> *The LORD will send a blessing on your barns and on everything you put your hand to. The LORD your God will bless you in the land he is giving you.*
>
> *Deuteronomy 28:8 NIV*

Because we are tithers, all of the nations will call us blessed and everything we set our hands to will prosper.

> *Lord, thank You that I am blessed. Thank You that I dwell in the land of plenty. I am financially secure. I have surplus and am successful in all that I set my hands to do. Father, thank You that I am dwelling in a delightful place and I am satisfied in the things of God, in Jesus' Name. Amen.* ☽☾

21 FINANCIAL INTEGRITY

> *These men lie in wait for their own blood; they waylay only themselves! Such is the end of all who go after ill-gotten gain; it takes away the lives of those who get it.*
>
> *Proverbs 1:18-19 NIV*

To operate in financial integrity means to guard and protect our motives while looking for gain in our lives. Some people have financial gain, but they do not have true prosperity. Gain alone is not holy. Do not be deceived into thinking that because you have financial accumulation, you also have God's approval on your life. The verses above warn that there is a type of gain that leads to sure destruction.

An example of this is seen of the life of Ahab. Ahab desired and coveted another man's property. (Covetousness means that we not only *want* what someone else has, but we want it *at their expense.*) Ahab allowed himself to be ruled by his emotions, and they determined his actions. He became disappointed and downcast when he didn't get want he wanted.

One reason for his fall was Ahab's ungrateful attitude. He was king, yet he still desired another man's vineyard. Not only was he ungrateful, but after he finally got his desire, he despised the rebuke of the God's prophet. When we look at the Word of God and see correction concerning our finances, we must be obedient.

Many men have been blessed with tremendous financial gain in the world. They have good intentions, but unfortunately, they do not always follow through with obeying God's Word. They continue living and handling their money the way they always have, and they lose everything, including their families. They think that because they have financial gain, God must be approving of their lifestyles, but they are deceived.

Do not think that financial gain means you have God's approval. God is looking to bless those who walk in obedience to His Word. Those who obey will not only receive the blessings of God's prosperity, but they will have the assurance of God's favor in their lives.

Lord, thank You that there is a way that I can
walk in financial integrity and be blessed. I can
be prosperous. I don't have to desire another
man's goods or covet what another man has in life
and want it at his expense. There is more than
enough blessing in Your kingdom for me. You are
the God of abundance. Lord, I thank You that I
can do everything I do by faith, and I can be
prosperous through obedience, in Jesus' Name.
Amen. ◑◐

22 WISDOM IN FINANCES

My son, if thou wilt receive my words, and hide
my commandments with thee; So that thou incline
thine ear unto wisdom, and apply thine heart to
understanding; Yea, if thou criest after knowledge,
and liftest up thy voice for understanding; If thou
seekest her as silver, and searchest for her as for
hid treasures; Then shalt thou understand the fear
of the LORD, and find the knowledge of God.
                              Proverbs 2:1-5 NIV

God tells us that we can ask for insight and understanding
when it comes to our personal finances.

According to I Corinthians 2:12, we have access to the
counsel of the Holy Spirit. God has given us the Holy
Spirit to advise us in every area of our lives. Understanding
is a far greater commodity than silver and gold. Silver and
gold are simply by-products of understanding.

In other words, *knowing how* to make a million dollars is
better than *winning* a million dollars. If we win a million
dollars, one million dollars is our reward. If we know how
to make a million dollars, however, we have the ability to
make a million dollars more than once.

We should seek God's understanding and wisdom in all that we do. God's wisdom and knowledge are found in His Word. If we will commit to study His Word and ask the Holy Spirit to reveal its truths to us, we will be richly rewarded and have abundant supply.

Lord, thank You that You bless me and give me Your wisdom and understanding when it comes to my finances. I thank You that You are very concerned about what I do and that I achieve success with integrity. I commit myself to the study of Your Word and I ask the Holy Spirit to reveal Your wisdom to me in every realm. I thank You for giving me divine understanding, in Jesus' Name. Amen. ◗◖

23 REAPING THE BLESSINGS OF HEAVEN

Honour the LORD with thy substance, and with the firstfruits of all thine increase: So shall thy barns be filled with plenty, and thy presses shall burst out with new wine.

Proverbs 3:9-10

Honoring God with the tithe is the highest purpose of our wealth. With the tithe, we worship the Lord and reflect our gratitude for all He has done. By giving Him the firstfruits of all our income, our tithe signifies that the Lord is the first priority in our lives.

A good man out of the good treasure of the heart bringeth forth good things: and an evil man out of the evil treasure bringeth forth evil things.

Matthew 12:35

What we have stored up is what we will draw from. Many people walk in ignorance concerning their evil ways. They think they can sow seeds of disobedience and still avoid crop failure. This is not the case. A man always reaps what he sows.

If we are depositing our tithe into the kingdom of God, we are able to draw blessings from the windows of Heaven. We are able to draw from a source that is higher than the world's economy and our barns will be filled with plenty and our presses will burst with divine overflow.

> *Father, I reflect that You are the first priority of my life and I offer my tithes in worship to You. I have stored up my finances in Your kingdom and the windows of Heaven are open to me. Thank You that You have blessed and prospered me. I can draw from Your storehouses and I don't have to depend on this world's economy. Your supernatural goodness is upon my finances, in Jesus' Name. Amen.*

24 SEEKING WISDOM

> *Wisdom is supreme; therefore get wisdom.*
> *Though it cost all you have, get understanding.*
> *Proverbs 4:7 NIV*

Because we are God's children, we have access to the source of all knowledge and understanding. Wisdom is the key to success, and we need to constantly seek it—not just one time—but all the time, in every decision that we make.

Acts chapter eight illustrates the importance of seeking knowledge. In the story, Queen Candace of Ethiopia entrusted all of her money and wealth to her chief financial advisor. He was a very intelligent man who sought knowledge from the Word of God. As he traveled along the road to Jerusalem on his way to worship in the Temple, he read a passage from the Book of Isaiah. This servant was seeking after greater understanding, and God supernaturally sent his answer to him by sending Philip to run after his chariot.

Like the Ethiopian eunuch, we need to seek knowledge in the Word of God, look for wise counsel from men of God, and apply it to our hearts. If we're looking for increase, we should not run after money. If we will run after wisdom, money will run after us.

> *Lord, thank You that Your Word is true. I thank You that I will be blessed as I seek understanding from its pages. Thank You also for sending wise men and women of God into my life to speak to me and to give me godly counsel as I pursue Your direction. Thank You that I will grow spiritually and have financial increase accordingly, in Jesus' Name. Amen.*

25 FREEDOM FROM DEBT

> *My son, if you have put up security for your neighbor, if you have struck hands in pledge for another, if you have been trapped by what you said, ensnared by the words of your mouth, then do this, my son, to free yourself, since you have fallen into your neighbor's hands: Go and humble yourself; press your plea with your neighbor! Allow no sleep to your eyes, no slumber to your eyelids. Free yourself, like a gazelle from the hand of the hunter, like a bird from the snare of the fowler.*
>
> *Proverbs 6:1-5 NIV*

God has given us the supernatural ability to free ourselves from binding agreements with integrity. In II Kings 6:4-7, this ability is illustrated. The prophets needed to enlarge their meeting place. One of the workers constructing the larger facility had an ax he was using to chop down a tree. With one of the blows, the iron ax head slipped off of its handle and fell into a nearby body of water. Unfortunately the ax head was borrowed and the worker was greatly distressed. Although it seemed like there was no hope, Elisha did a miracle. The ax head surfaced, and the worker was able to return it and free himself from his binding agreement.

God is concerned with the financial agreements we enter into, and He will help us to live up to the terms of any contract with integrity. Sometimes, our laws are very liberal concerning contracts and spoken agreements, and because of this, we may view them flippantly. Legal contracts are not just laws of the land; they are also binding on us concerning the laws of God. For this reason, we need to be extremely careful that we abide by the rules of any contract we enter into. Our word should be our bond.

The principle of the tithe is a law of God that is like any contract we may enter into. God will keep His Word concerning the tithe and pour out His blessings on us, but we must live up to our end of the agreement faithfully in order to partake of its benefits. God's Word is true, and we should always maintain truth and integrity in all of our dealings in order to be His witnesses to the world.

> *Lord, thank You that You have given me the opportunity to be freed from financial pressure. You've given me a supernatural ability to walk with integrity concerning my finances. The tithe is Your way to bring the blessing of Heaven upon my life and all my dealings. Thank You, Lord, for pouring out avenues of blessing to release me from my debts with integrity so I might be Your witness, in Jesus' Name. Amen.*

26 RIGHTEOUS THINKING IN FINANCES

I walk in the way of righteousness, along the
paths of justice, bestowing wealth on those who
love me and making their treasuries full.
                              Proverbs 8:20-21 NIV

One of the wealthiest men in Australia is well known for saying, "The decisions that you make are yours—good or bad—yours to enjoy or yours to endure."

Clearly, wisdom is vital in making financial decisions. In fact, financial wisdom always agrees with righteous thinking. If we operate according to righteousness, wealth, riches, honor and victory will be our reward.

If any of you lacks wisdom, he should ask God,
who gives generously to all without finding fault,
and it will be given to him.
                              James 1:5 NIV

God wants to give us the wisdom to make good decisions. Wisdom is not about natural position or possessions. Even though he had already been made the King of Israel, Solomon still asked God for the wisdom to lead God's people (II Chronicles 1:10). God was pleased with Solomon's request and He blessed him, not only with wisdom, but also with abundant wealth. When we seek the kingdom of God and His righteousness first, material possessions will be given to us as well (Matthew 6:33).

We cannot be fooled into believing more money is the answer to our troubles. Righteous thinking is the answer; money is merely a by-product. If we think righteously concerning our finances, we will put God's kingdom first in everything that we do. We will devote the firstfruits of our increase to the Lord in the tithe, and then we will be able to boldly request His wisdom to guide us in every decision we make.

*Lord, I seek after You and Your righteousness
because You are the one and only source of
wisdom. You said that I could ask You for wisdom
and that You would give it to me generously
without finding fault. I want a renewed mind full
of righteous thoughts concerning my finances. I
don't want to be deceived by wealth or the things
of this world, but I want to always seek Your ways
in the area of my finances. Thank You for giving
me wisdom, in Jesus' Name. Amen.* ☉☽

27 HONORING GOD IN TITHES AND OFFERINGS

*And the Jews' passover was at hand, and Jesus
went up to Jerusalem, And found in the temple
those that sold oxen and sheep and doves, and the
changers of money sitting: And when he had
made a scourge of small cords, he drove them all
out of the temple, and the sheep, and the oxen;
and poured out the changers' money, and
overthrew the tables; And said unto them that sold
doves, Take these things hence; make not my
Father's house an house of merchandise. And his
disciples remembered that it was written, The zeal
of thine house hath eaten me up.*

John 2:13-17

This passage of scripture shows a characteristic of Jesus
that we are not accustomed to thinking about, but it is
important that we clearly understand these verses, or we
may misinterpret Jesus' actions. The Bible teaches that the
offering is a connection between fallen man and our
Heavenly Father. As a result of sin, Jesus came to restore
that relationship.

Ideally, in Bible times people were to raise their own cattle
and livestock, treat them with loving care and offer only the

very best in worshiping God. But the first chapter of the Book of Malachi reveals how the people began to dishonor God in the area of giving. They no longer offered their best, but instead they offered blemished animals. They brought God the blind, the sick and the lame from their flocks—not the first and the best as He had commanded them.

For the people of Jerusalem, presenting the offering at the Temple became a time of disrespect, rather than a time of honor to God. The people treated their relationship with the Lord as something not worthy of their highest and best efforts. But Jesus demonstrated that God is zealous about our offerings.

God offered His highest and best sacrifice—His only Son— to restore us to a right relationship to Him. Shouldn't we also offer Him our first and our best?

> *Thank You, Heavenly Father, that You gave everything to restore me to a right relationship with You. You gave Your Son, Jesus Christ, to redeem me and to save me from my sin. I will not take our relationship lightly, Lord. I will worship You with my highest and best offerings as a tangible expression of my gratitude for what Jesus has done for me. I love You, Lord, in Jesus' Name. Amen.* ◉◉

28 EXPRESSING YOUR FAITH IN FINANCES

> *And Jesus sat over against the treasury, and beheld how the people cast money into the treasury: and many that were rich cast in much. And there came a certain poor widow, and she threw in two mites, which make a farthing.*
> *Mark 12:41-42*

Mark 12:41-42 teaches us several things. We've already mentioned how it shows us that Jesus takes notice of what we give. He is ever watchful of our tithes and offerings. He even noticed this woman who gave only 1/40 of a cent.

Another thing this passage reveals is that if our offering is significant to us, it is significant to God. The wealthy people mentioned in these scriptures gave only a fraction of their wealth—probably only a very small fraction. Their offering amounts may have been large, but in comparison to their total wealth, they were very insignificant. The widow, however, gave her complete wealth—an offering worthy of commendation by God.

Hebrews 4:12 tells us that the Word of God is sharper than any double-edged sword. It judges the thoughts and attitudes of our hearts. The offerings we give are expressions of our heart toward God and expressions of our faith in His Word. If we will give significantly, according to what we have, we will reap significantly and have the approval of God. Even though the check we write may be small in comparison to those around us, God is not looking at the dollar signs, He is looking at our hearts.

Lord, I thank You that I have an opportunity to worship You in the area of giving. Thank You that You take notice of my offerings. Lord, I don't have to suffer under condemnation because I may not have been able to give a large sum of money. I will not misjudge my gift by comparing it to what others may have given. Thank You, Lord, that You see my heart. Thank You for prospering me and pouring out a blessing on me that I cannot contain. Thank You for being faithful to Your Word, in Jesus' Name. Amen.

29 THE LAW OF DILIGENCE

Whatever you do, work at it with all your heart, as working for the Lord, not for men, since you know that you will receive an inheritance from the Lord as a reward. It is the Lord Christ you are serving.
                                        Colossians 3:23-24 NIV

For even when we were with you, we gave you this rule: "If a man will not work, he shall not eat." We hear that some among you are idle. They are not busy; they are busybodies. Such people we command and urge in the Lord Jesus Christ to settle down and earn the bread they eat.
                                        II Thessalonians 3:10-12 NIV

In order to prosper, we must obey the principles of prosperity. One of these principles is the law of diligence.

Proverbs 28:19 says, **"He who works his land will have abundant food, but the one who chases fantasies will have his fill of poverty"** (NIV). The law of diligence—equally important as tithing and planting seeds—teaches us that we must work, if we want to have abundance. We cannot expect to have prosperity, if we are not good stewards in our jobs. A job is not just a career or a source of income. It is a "vocation." The word *vocation* comes from the root word *vocal*, and it literally means *"the divine spoken word over your life."*

We should be employed following the plan that God spoke over our lives at the time of our conception. He wants us to be blessed, and He is more than willing to bless us if we will obey His principles. He promises to prosper everything we put our hands to and to give us increase, however, the law of prosperity will only work in our lives, if we work. If we want to see abundance, we need to be about our Father's business.

Lord, I thank You for the opportunity to work Your Word. You watch over Your Word to see it performed in my life. Your Word will not return unto You void. It will accomplish what You've sent it to accomplish. Lord, You've given me the promise of prosperity, and I will respond with diligent action. I thank You that with corresponding faith, I will prosper in everything I put my hand to, in Jesus' Name. Amen. ⊙⊙

30 FLOURISHING IN THE WORD

The righteous will flourish like a palm tree, they will grow like a cedar of Lebanon; planted in the house of the LORD, they will flourish in the courts of our God. They will still bear fruit in old age, they will stay fresh and green, proclaiming, "The LORD is upright; he is my Rock, and there is no wickedness in him."

Psalm 92:12-15 NIV

Without a doubt, it is God's will for the righteous to flourish.

The righteous should have growth. We should be expanding, increasing and ever learning. We should be flourishing in our God. The Lord promises that if we abide in His Word and stay planted in His house, we will grow.

Drawing sustenance from God and His Word is the only way we can bear fruit. Without Jesus, we will not flourish. He is the divine Seed God planted into humanity, and it is through Him that we will prosper. If we want to flourish in the courts of our God, the psalmist stresses the importance of our being planted in the house of God—that means a good church where we can hear His Word and learn about Him.

If we abide in His Word and keep our feet firmly planted in His house, the Bible says we will still bear fruit in our old age. Others around us may grow weary and dim, but we will stay fresh and green. We will continue to grow like a mighty tree and the fruit we produce will nourish those around us.

> *Thank You, Lord, that I can flourish. I'm grafted into Your family and I draw sustenance out of Christ. Even when others around me grow weary and faint, I will bear much fruit and stay fresh and green. My feet are planted in Your house and my home is blessed. I have increase in every realm, in Jesus' Name. Amen.* ☉☉

31 TRUE PROSPERITY

> *For ye know the grace of our Lord Jesus Christ, that, though he was rich, yet for your sakes he became poor, that ye through his poverty might be rich.*
>
> *II Corinthians 8:9*

We are redeemed from the curse of poverty through the grace that is found in Christ. God has a grace for us in the area of finances and a promise of true prosperity.

Prosperity means more than an accumulation of possessions. It means having a sense of security. As a child, I grew up in Oklahoma, and we had many possessions. We had land, livestock, a couple of homes, businesses and such, but I never once felt that we were prosperous. In fact, I always thought of our family as somewhat poor because there was never a sense of security in our home.

In spite of sin, progress, increase and ungodly gain may still be achieved in the world. In order to have true prosperity,

A Devotional Guide To God's Blessing   151

though, one must have a relationship with Jesus Christ. We cannot have security without God. True prosperity reflects divine approval, and is found only by seeking God.

Obedient believers frame their lives, comfort and wealth with a complete dependence on God, just as faithful Abraham did. Abraham looked to the Lord in faith and continually walked toward Him in obedience. God, Himself, was the hope that Abraham pressed toward. We, too, must continually walk toward God and claim our redemption from poverty, sickness and spiritual death.

If you have never accepted Jesus Christ as your personal Lord and Savior, you cannot achieve true prosperity. The things of this world—money, possessions and success—can never bring you the true peace and wealth of a life of complete dependence and faith in God's plan. No matter what you possess, if you don't have Christ at the center of your life, your spirit is poor beyond measure.

If you have never accepted Jesus Christ as your Savior and turned your life over to His Lordship, I encourage you to do it now! Don't wait to enter into a relationship with God that will bring you spiritual riches untold. It is only when we seek Him first and truly live for Him that the blessing of God is added to our lives.

To accept Jesus as your Lord, pray this prayer out loud:

> *Heavenly Father, I come to You to submit my life and my heart to Your plan. I believe that You sent Your Son, Jesus Christ, to die for my sins. I need Your forgiveness. I believe that You raised Jesus from the dead and I now boldly declare that Jesus is my Lord. I commit myself to live in obedience to You and Your Word all the days of my life. Thank You that Jesus lives in my heart. Help me to follow after You from this day forward, in Jesus' Name, Amen.*

As we walk closer in our relationship to Christ each day, we will achieve secure and lasting prosperity in every sense of the word.

> *Lord, I thank You that my prosperity is so much more than accumulating possessions. True prosperity means that my journey will go well, that I will be a blessing to those I come into contact with, and that when I see a need, I'm able to meet it. As I continue to grow in my relationship with You, I thank You for helping me to receive Your blessings, so that I might be able to sow even more into the preaching of the Gospel. Thank You for redeeming me from the curse of poverty, sickness and spiritual death, and for giving me true prosperity, in Jesus' Name. Amen.*

ABOUT THE AUTHOR

Neil Kennedy discovered the truths about *God's Currency* and *The Seven Laws Which Govern Divine Increase And Order* out of necessity, from the principles he found in God's Word and from his own personal experience.

Neil worked as a heavy-machine operator in a coalmine in Oklahoma before attending Central Bible College in Springfield, Missouri, where he majored in Pastoral Studies. Working his way through college, Neil discovered that even his job as a salesman in a local carwash would give him insight into God's Word and His principles.

After finishing college and serving as a youth minister, Neil felt the Lord calling him to step out and pioneer Eastern Shore Christian Center in Mobile, Alabama. Growing the congregation from five people to 500, God then led Neil to step down from his position as Senior Pastor to become Executive Pastor at Church On The Move in Tulsa, Oklahoma. His experiences there allowed him to help develop the inner-workings of one of America's fastest-growing "mega-churches," where he was responsible for the entire pastoral care department, overseeing the needs of more than 10,000 members each week.

In 2001, armed with instruction from the Word and the practical knowledge he had gained, Neil once again felt the Lord directing him to pioneer a church. Obeying the Lord's call, he stepped out and founded Celebrate Family Church, in Orlando, Florida.

Neil's practical insight and straight-forward communication style have inspired thousands to take the necessary steps to realize their God-given potential. Neil's expertise makes him a highly-sought-after speaker and consultant to churches and businesses alike, and to anyone who wants to increase and achieve all that God has for them.

Neil now travels each week, ministering in churches and conducting seminars across America. Neil's burning desire is to challenge pastors, church congregations, and individuals to fulfill God's purposes for themselves.

Neil has served on numerous boards, committees, and strategy forums, including the U.S. Missions Board, the Decade Of Harvest Task Force, the Evangelism Task Force, and the Dove-Award-winning musical group 4-Him.

Grace To Grow, the Ministry of Neil Kennedy, has the mission of teaching, equipping and funding church endeavors. His specialties include:

- Church Planting—developing and helping new works to go from the ground up,

- "Turn-Around" Churches—ministering to churches who've let tradition slow their momentum and find themselves irrelevant in today's world, and

- "Next-Level" churches—assisting pastors who, for whatever reason, have hit a barrier in their growth they just can't seem to break through.

Neil has also helped launch an e-marketing company, called "ChurchTour 360," which aids churches in developing positive public relations images in their communities.

Neil and his wife, Kay, have three children, Alexandra, Chase, and Courtney, and they reside in Fairhope, Alabama.

For more information about Neil Kennedy Ministries or to schedule Neil for a meeting, please visit www.NeilKennedyMinistries.com.

43798157R00092

Made in the USA
Middletown, DE
19 May 2017